CHERRY PICKING

If the Cherries Aren't Low Enough...Get a Ladder!

MIKE JACKSON

Editor: Emily Rogers
Illustrations: Carlton Primm

Copyright © 2008 Mike Jackson

ISBN: 1-4392-2074-3
ISBN-13: 9781439220740

Visit www.booksurge.com to order additional copies.

CONTENTS

INTRODUCTION

The true count of how many jobs that are lost each year as a result of Cherry Picking may never be known, but the estimates are staggering. Cherry Picking has not only caused the loss of countless jobs, but even worse, it has caused companies to permanently close their doors. The information in this book may have saved them.

Recent research has revealed that Cherry Picking is practiced by every Sales Professional selling every product and *every* service. It is simply a matter *of to what degree* that each Sales Professional Cherry Picks.

I want to make clear the term "Cherry Picking", for all of the intent and purposes of how I will use it in this book. You are probably familiar with the phrase, "If the cherries are not low enough…" In this book, Cherry Picking is defined as when a Sales Professional chooses to either work a customer to the fullest extent… *or not to.*

In other words, Cherry Picking is when a Sales Professional chooses <u>when</u> and to <u>whom</u> they are going to perform their complete presentation. The decision of whether to work the customer or not is influenced by thoughts in the Sales Professional's mind. It is precisely these thoughts and what fuels these thoughts that will be explored in this book.

In the worst cases of Cherry Picking, Sales Professionals have allowed fully ready, willing, and able customers to walk without receiving a complete presentation. Cherry Picking thoughts are powerful and can manipulate the Sales Professional's decision to cut their presentation short — and let fully qualified customers walk, resulting in another lost sale.

Current estimates of the true cost of Cherry Picking are staggering. However, on the flip side, this means there is an incredible opportunity for you. By applying the material in this book and by conquering your selective selling habits, you will substantially increase your income.

In the little over 8 years that it took to do research for this book, I traveled to 68 major U.S. cities. Through my sales training company, Progressive Insights, Inc., I personally walked into thousands of businesses across North America and evaluated thousands of Sales Professional's presentations. I reviewed the Sales Professional's rapport building and qualifying efforts, and I evaluated their overall desire to take control and "work me".

For many years, I traveled sometimes three or four weeks out of the month, evaluating Sales Presentations on a national level. Although I observed some slight variables in local cultures (for example, folks in Salt Lake City were a little different than the folks in Miami) I found an overwhelming common denominator in all of the Sales Professionals that I encountered.

I will not say that all salespeople are the same because that is definitely not true. However, all Sales Professionals are human, and there is a simple and basic human nature that affects all Sales Professionals. It is this human nature that we will identify and understand in the following pages. Armed with this insight along with some others, we will be able to take the necessary actions to eliminate Cherry Picking. As a result, you will start generating more sales.

The information in this book is a culmination of hundreds of conversations with business owners, sales managers, sales trainers, and sales coaches from across North America. From Seattle to San Diego, from Baltimore to Miami, and a lot of cities in between, I met with top professionals in sales management and discussed Cherry Picking with them.

In addition to consulting with sales managers and trainers, I also spoke to the people on the front line; I spoke to hundreds of Sales Professionals about Cherry Picking as well. I share this information in the following chapters.

I want to make it clear that this is not a "how to sell" book. In fact, without the knowledge of some selling fundamentals, it may be hard for you to identify with this material.

In order for you to receive the maximum results from this book, you must already own these simple, yet paramount, beliefs:

1. The belief that *Better Presentations Generate More Sales.*

2. The belief that you must use the proper *selling strategy* with each individual customer and speak to them in their world of listening.

3. The belief that in order to generate the maximum amount of sales possible, you have to execute your selling strategy and perform a complete, planned presentation *on every customer*... unless they stop you.

If you own these beliefs, then clearly you are already on your way to the top. The material in this book will get you there faster.

If you do not own these beliefs, you have not yet quite arrived. You simply just don't know *what you just don't know*. Perhaps you are just beginning your sales career and do not yet understand what is necessary for you to reach your greatest potential.

If, by chance, you are just beginning your sales career, there is very good news for you. You do not have to read hundreds of Sales Training books to become knowledgeable on the fundamentals of sales. The reason is that most of the information on the fundamentals of selling is very similar; it is all related. You only need to read a couple of those books to become knowledgeable about the fundamentals of selling.

There are countless books written on one fundamental, universal selling strategy, which consists of: The Greeting, Qualifying, Demonstrating, and Closing. At the core, all of the materials written about this fundamental strategy are the same. The variety of ways in which the books are written allow you to find a format that you like and can best relate to.

While one book on this fundamental strategy may explain that you have to be friendly during *"The Greeting"*, another book might say that you need to have a great *"First Impression"*. Whether it's called *"The Greeting"*, *"The First Impression"*, or the elaborate *"Initial Contact"* makes no difference; it is all the same concept, just written with different words.

However, I believe that the real key in Sales Training is not how they write about the previous fundamental selling strategy; the real key to success in Sales Training is how to get

Sales Professionals to *own it and use it* on *every customer*. This would mean that they would live a life of selling…Cherry Picking-Free.

Before starting my own sales training company, I spent over 20 years selling millions of dollars of different products and services. In the last 10 years of my selling career, I won numerous Sales Achievement Awards in the New Home Industry. Although most people would say that I experienced a rather successful selling career, I wish I was handed a check today for all of my lost sales due to my own Cherry Picking. In other words, it takes one to know one.

The key to every individual's growth, both personal and professional, hinges on the ability for the individual to internalize and self-reflect on their current ability, identify where they could improve, choose actions necessary to improve, and move forward with those actions with integrity. This book will ask you to self-reflect on some core issues that affect your Sales Presentation habits. You will:

*Identify with your internal representations about your customers that result in the specific actions you take in some of your Sales Presentations.

*Understand your current motivation level and learn how to raise it.

*Become in tune with your selling style and selling personality type and recognize how your personality traits translate into your Sales Presentations.

Once you identify your current selling habits, you will learn how Cherry Picking thoughts can influence you and cost you sales. This book will not only identify those costly thoughts that influence you to Cherry Pick; more importantly, this book will provide you with specific actions to take so you can conquer those thoughts.

This book will launch your sales career to the highest level. Simply being armed with this new knowledge will boost your confidence level. After learning to control your Cherry Picking thoughts, you will generate an abundance of additional sales, and you will feel the highest level possible of self-satisfaction about your sales achievements.

Your additional influx of income will allow you to move your lifestyle up one notch or two. And if they haven't yet passed a law against it in your state…you can save a bunch of money. At any rate, you will like being at the top of your Sales Game.

I lightened the tone of some of the material that follows. It's O.K. to laugh. In fact, I hope that you not only laugh as you read about what others may have done, but that you identify and laugh at some of the things that you may have done as well. Sometimes a little humor can allow a point to really sink in. The point is – that you get the point.

If you are ready, please read on.

ONE

Early History of Cherry Picking

The true count of how many jobs that are lost each year as a result of Cherry Picking may never be known. It is estimated that millions of Sales Professionals currently Cherry Pick. In fact, studies have revealed that Cherry Picking is practiced by *every* Sales Professional selling *every* product and *every* service. It's simply a matter of *to what degree* that each Sales Professional Cherry Picks.

The question is, how much does it cost you? In a later chapter, we will explore the true cost of your Cherry Picking.

I want to make clear the term "Cherry Picking" as it will be used in this book. Cherry Picking is when a Sales Professional chooses either to pursue a sale, to work a customer to the fullest extent, or *not to*. In very simple terms, Cherry Picking is when a Sales Professional chooses <u>when</u> and <u>to whom</u> they are going to sell.

In the worst cases, Sales Professionals allow fully ready, willing, and able customers to walk, simply because the Sales Professional chose <u>not</u> to perform a complete, planned presentation and pursue the sale.

I have done extensive research on the reasons *why* people Cherry Pick, and a rather long list of reasons has been discovered. You will learn about the Cherry Picking "reasons" later. They will be revealed to you in a way that will allow you to remember them and explain them to fellow Sales Professionals.

At this time, the true origin of Cherry Picking is still a mystery. The experts cannot seem to agree on the exact period of history in which Cherry Picking began. Long before a cash system for purchasing goods and services became a global phenomenon, people used the "barter system", a fancy name for trading or exchanging, to acquire things they needed.

It is rumored that way back in the beginning of these bartering days, that somewhere in the Middle East, one person chose <u>not</u> to trade with a potential customer. The exact reason is not clear. The rumor is that they did not like the camel the person rode up on. But because bartering goes back thousands of years, and without many written records of such deals, the experts may never agree on the true origin of Cherry Picking.

The exact whereabouts of the original act of Cherry Picking in North America may never be known, however, it is speculated that it may have occurred early in the 17th century.

Rumor has it that Cherry Picking started with an event that happened with a family that settled in North America — the "New World". The family lived in a small village with other European settlers in what is now known as Virginia.

Early on, when the first settlers came to America, they bartered with the native Indians that had already been living in this New World. The new settlers had intriguing gadgets to trade with the Indians. They had things like guns and whiskey. In return, the Indians, who lived a self-sufficient lifestyle, offered the settlers some basic essentials for their survival. The Indians had things like corn and blankets. It was a win-win deal for both.

Early settlers had things like guns and whiskey. Indians could barter with blankets and corn. It was a win-win deal for both.

Everything was going well between the settlers and the Indians. Perhaps this very same village was where the first "Thanksgiving Dinner" was shared. With winter soon approaching, the bartering season was about to close, and something terrible was about to happen.

One of the settlers desperately needed some blankets. The settler had made some of the best whiskey, and he wanted to trade it for some blankets. An Indian came around with some blankets that he had made to trade with, and he met with the previously mentioned settler who had the whiskey.

The Indian made a complete, planned presentation on his blankets. Many of the other settlers had already traded with him. But when it was the settler's turn to talk about his whiskey, for some unknown reason, the settler chose <u>not</u> to do a complete presentation on his whiskey. The settler said nothing to the Indian about the quality of his whiskey. Although the settler used the highest quality ingredients and spared no expense in producing his whiskey, he mentioned nothing about it.

The settler's friends knew that he had a good presentation, because at other times they saw him do it. They saw him explain in a very positive way about the higher quality ingredients that he used and how they compared to what other settlers in other villages used. His fellow settlers had heard him previously mention that the quality ingredients he used made a profound difference in the smoothness of his whiskey. Everyone knew that the settler could do a *complete, planned presentation*, because they had heard it before.

But this time, however, the settler mentioned nothing about his quality ingredients. He offered no taste as a sample. For some unknown reason, he chose <u>not</u> to do a *complete presentation*.

The Indian did not trade. The settler received no blankets.

All of the other settlers had already completed their successful bartering with the Indian. They were all set up with their much needed blankets. That fall, no other Indians came around.

Winter arrived.

Without the blankets, the settler's children nearly died. It was a very long, cold winter. If it wasn't for a team effort with friends pitching in, the settler's family may not have survived.

The other settlers asked him, "Why did you not perform a complete presentation on your whiskey, and barter your whiskey for some blankets?"

The settler replied, "I just knew that *another Indian* I had talked to before would "*be-back*" — but he never did."

Perhaps Cherry Picking started out as a very simple thought in North American culture. Perhaps a simple thought that originated in just one individual's mind. And perhaps, similar to a flu-like virus, it spread from one person to another. My studies show that the elders are most affected.

The next chapter will update you on all of the current data.

Knowledge is Power.

Chapter Highlights

- **Companies have closed their doors forever because of Cherry Picking.**

- **In modern times, Cherry Picking causes Sales Professionals to let ready, willing, and able customers walk without seeing a complete sales presentation.**

TWO

Current Data

Cherry Picking thoughts are very strong. They are very difficult to control, let alone eliminate them entirely. In fact, some Sales Professionals are simply overtaken by their Cherry Picking thoughts, and in slower times it can be devastating for them. Due to their steady loss of income, these unfortunate Sales Professionals are forced to keep moving their lifestyle down a level, as their sales career dies a slow, painful death.

Vast resources have been invested in battling Cherry Picking. Although there have been some giant leaps forward in controlling Cherry Picking, a couple of major hurdles still remain. One hurdle is that almost no Sales Professional seeks help. If you were to attempt taking a survey, you would find that most all Sales Professionals keep their Cherry Picking thoughts confidential.

Perhaps Sales Professionals might feel embarrassed if they told someone about their Cherry Picking thoughts, so they do not let anyone know that they have them. They just keep it to themselves.

Simply put, we can't help them if they don't ask. Hopefully, old-fashioned word of mouth will happen about this book, and those people in need will take the keys away from their egos. Hopefully, Sales Professionals will spend the equivalent of one lunch for something that will make them thousands - we can only hope. It seems that in recognition of the sales ego, managers are buying this book for their Sales Professionals. It is becoming a "must read".

Some Sales Professionals may feel embarrassed if they talk about their Cherry Picking thoughts. Others actually brag about it.

Another challenge in getting help to Sales Professionals in need is that the majority of Sales Professionals infected with Cherry Picking thoughts only show slight symptoms. They operate at an almost normal level of sales performance. From a mystery shop, their Sales Presentation scores fall in the 60s and 70s out of 100 range. They consistently post sales results that fall in the middle to the bottom of their Sales Team. They work at a company for a while and just go unnoticed. Then they leave.

Most customers just look at these Sales Professionals as being very "laid back". Customers refer to them as, "just not aggressive at all". Of course, only lay-downs ever buy from "laid back" Sales Professionals. The lay-downs just wait for the Sales Professional to be finished with their mediocre Sales Presentation, and then they ask, "If I wanted to buy it, what would I need to do?" The Sales Professional then just simply "takes the order."

My studies show that Cherry Picking thoughts are very similar to flu-like or computer-like viruses, in the fact that just like there are variations in flu or computer viruses, there are variations in Cherry Picking. If you wanted to, you could refer to it as "The Cherry Picking Virus". And there are very different and distinct variations of Cherry Picking.

My extensive research reveals that different Sales Professionals give different reasons for Cherry Picking. Since Sales Professionals show very different symptoms, this could lead you to believe that there are different strains of the Cherry Picking Virus.

Again, as mentioned previously, most Sales Professionals do not tell anyone that they have any Cherry Picking thoughts. They just keep it to themselves and perform at a mediocre level of performance. They are hard to help.

However, there is another group of Sales Professionals that I found and they are very different than the ones who keep their Cherry Picking to themselves. This group shows very different symptoms that are easily detected. Instead of hiding their thoughts about Cherry Picking, these Sales Professionals actually brag about it! They boast to all of their friends and co-workers that they Cherry Pick! They brag to their co-workers of how they choose to <u>not</u> work with a certain type of person; they say they just "blow them off". These braggers freely announce that they do not work with entire cultures of people. They brag about not working with entire races, cultures, and religious groups, and otherwise stereotype people in broad perspectives of however they see justified. These Sales Professionals actually brag as if their actions were something to be proud of!

Sales Trainers are really challenged with the group of Sales Professionals that brag about their Cherry Picking for one simple reason: why would those sick Sales Professionals need help with generating more sales and increasing their income – if they don't feel sick? They don't think they need any help because they don't think anything is wrong with them.

Maybe this book will help them. We can only hope.

As mentioned earlier, studies have shown that Cherry Picking affects *every* Sales Professional, selling *every* product and *every* service. It's just a matter of *to what degree* that they Cherry Pick, and more importantly, how much it ends up costing them.

We are not only learning more about how Cherry Picking is passed from one Sales Professional to another, but we are also learning how Sales Professionals deal with it. Recent studies show that it may depend on each individual's genetic make-up, as well as their environment. It is a challenge to determine which plays the largest role, and I am performing double-blind studies as of this writing.

It appears that some Sales Professionals are simply blessed. Their immune system is stronger than others. It seems that they were just *born* with great sales abilities. They do not practice much Cherry Picking at all. It's as if it were in their DNA to perform a complete, planned presentation to every customer.

Their peers are envious.

Perhaps the way they were raised also helps these Sales Professionals to sell "Cherry Picking-Free." Perhaps their environment, the way they were brought up in the business, having the right mentor, etc., is the reason for their powerful ability to fight Cherry Picking. My studies reveal that how well these Sales Professionals control their thoughts directly relates to the degree that they Cherry Pick. They allow themselves to fight Cherry Picking thoughts. They tell themselves, "I have to do my Sales Presentation now; <u>it's my job</u>!" They put aside whatever they were doing, put on their Sales Professional's hat, and do their Sales Presentation like they were hired to do.

Most other Sales Professionals are not so fortunate.

The unfortunate ones do not have a strong immune system. Perhaps the way they were raised caused their mental immune system to not fully develop. Perhaps some previous life experience is anchored in their brain, and it prevents them from controlling their thoughts. They do not do their job, and they feel their reason for not doing it is perfectly justified. They think it's quite O.K. to not perform their complete presentation for whatever reason they choose at the time. And perhaps they watched their coworkers Cherry Pick, and in the short-term, their coworkers sold one or two customers by Cherry Picking, so it must be O.K. Cherry Picking appeared to work. It is frightening for business owners and managers to see that these unfortunate Sales Professionals make up the mass majority, and they need a strong prescription of something to help fight their mental illness.

For quite some time, the best prescription for Cherry Picking was known to be given by Sales Managers. When their sales dropped off, and the Sales Professional showed symptoms of not completing their presentations and not selling, the Sales Manager prescribed a heavy dose of, "Sell something now!"

Initial studies showed positive results from the "Sales Manager's Prescription". The effects were both immediate and impressive. After taking only one dose of the Sales Manager's Prescription, many Sales Professionals performed their next Sales Presentation much better. They showed no symptoms of any kind. It appeared that the Cherry Picking "virus" was gone.

But my later studies revealed a severe side-effect.

The Sales Manager's Prescription was shown to be highly addictive, and its effects only lasted for a short time. The prescription did indeed cause a chemical change in the brain, which in turn caused the Sales Professional to act differently. Unfortunately, however, that change was only short-lived.

In some isolated cases, I saw the change lasting for as long as several months, but that proved to be the exception. The majority of Sales Professionals showed that the Sales Manager's medicine lasted for a much shorter time.

In fact, there were cases where the Sales Manager's Prescription actually started to wear off *almost immediately* after it was taken. I saw one case where the Sales Manager dished out the medicine to the Sales Professional and watched them swallow it, but *immediately upon leaving the office of the Sales Manager*, the

> **The medicine started to wear off immediately upon leaving the Sales manager's office.**

effects of the medicine started to wear off. The Sales Professional did *not* perform a complete presentation on their *very next customer*.

Can you imagine how much company revenues are being lost from Cherry Picking? Remember, as I mentioned earlier, *every* Sales Professional Cherry Picks — it is simply a matter of *to what degree* that they do it.

Stop for a moment, and think about how many sales you may have lost as a result of Cherry Picking.

We will focus more on that later. Right now, let's go to the next chapter and clearly identify the distinct varieties of the Cherry Picking Virus and their different symptoms. This will help you identify what type you may have.

Chapter Highlights

• **Cherry Picking thoughts are very strong and difficult to control.**

• **We can't help a Sales Professional if they don't feel they need it.**

• **Sales coaches and trainers are extremely challenged to help Sales Professionals that brag about their Cherry Picking.**

• **The best known remedy for Cherry Picking was believed to be a dose of the "Sales Manager's Prescription", but it proved to be addictive and was short-lived.**

THREE

Virus #1 Type "Peek"

Similar to there being a variety of flu or computer viruses, there is more than one strain of the Cherry Picking Virus. I have identified at least two distinct varieties. And there is conclusive evidence that they are both highly contagious.

Research shows that Cherry Picking is easily passed from one Sales Professional to another. Some studies have shown that brand-new Sales Professionals enter a company or industry "Cherry Picking-Free." There is definitely a link between a Sales Professional's tenure and Cherry Picking.

Research reveals that brand-new Sales Professionals enter a company Cherry Picking-Free, then after working with a seasoned Sales Professional, the new Sales Professional starts Cherry Picking. Unfortunately, once infected with the Cherry Picking virus, the new Sales Professional has a slim-to-none chance at becoming a top producer. They never generate enough sales. No matter how hard they try to function with Cherry Picking, the newly infected Sales Professionals usually perform low enough that they either quit or get fired because of their lack of sales.

You need to understand the massive damage that Cherry Picking can do to your income potential. Most Sales Professionals are forced to live one or two lifestyles below their true potential because of their Cherry Picking.

> **The Peek Qualifying strain affects a Sales Professional's visual and cognitive processes.**

The following is the first variety of Cherry Picking that you will learn about.

This strain of the Cherry Picking Virus I call the *PEEK QUALIFYING* strain.

This Cherry Picking strain affects a Sales Professional's visual and cognitive processes. The Sales Professional does not see and think clearly. They see people and qualify them by the way they look. Then, they choose to either work the customer or not. They qualify people from just a quick *peek* of them.

In other words, when infected, the Sales Professional actually believes that their unmatched sales skills allow them to judge a customer's ability to buy – just by taking a quick *peek* at them.

I find it incredible that many Sales Professionals actually believe that their instant, visual assessment – their quick peek – is all that they need to determine a customer's desire and ability to buy. And based solely on that isolated, insignificant information, the Sales Professional will choose to *not* do a complete presentation.

Countless cases of this behavior have been witnessed. When these Sales Professionals are asked why they did not perform their complete, planned presentation to their customer, these Sales Professionals answer with conviction that they could "just tell" that the people were not going to buy, and that they "just *knew*" they would be wasting their time.

Clearly, the fact that ugly people have money throws most Sales Professionals for a loop. I don't know where they get it either, but I know that ugly people have money and cannot be blown-off.

This is a quick funny story that a friend of mine told me when I worked in new home sales; it exemplifies this type of Cherry Picking.

One weekend, my friend was working with his sales partner. At that time, they were working on an "alternating up" system. In other words, when one potential customer walked into the model home, one Sales Professional would help that person. Then, when the next customer walked in, it was the other Sales Professional's turn to work that customer, and so on. It was referred to as an "alternating up" system.

On that particular day, my friend and his sales partner had lost track of whose turn it was. They were not sure which of them should help the next customer when they came in. After a while, my friend said he saw some people pull up to the model home and get out of their car. He yelled to his sales partner, who was in the back of the model home, "Someone is coming in! Is it your up or mine?" His sales partner yelled back, "I don't know, I can't see them!"

I guess if she could have quickly *peeked* at them just before they walked in, she would have *known* they were qualified, so they would have been her up. If they didn't *look* good to her, I guess they were my friend's up!

As a savvy consumer, you could really play this to your advantage. If you were going to buy a big-ticket item like a new car or a new home, you could dress down. When you negotiated with the Sales Professional to lower their price, you could say, "I can only afford _____" (name your price). Your price would be valid in the mind of the Sales Professional, because after all, just look at you.

In fact, I can imagine the Sales Professional's call to his Sales Manager now: "No, boss, I can't get any more from them; I've worked them pretty hard. They just can't afford any more than this."

"I can't believe he fell for it."

Most Sales Professionals that catch this variation of Cherry Picking become removed from reality. It's simple — poll 100 *normal people*. Ask 100 normal people that *do not* work in sales this question:

"Do you believe that a Sales Professional has the ability to make a quick *peek* at someone, and determine that person's ability to buy a product or service?"

Out of 100 normal people that you ask, very few will answer yes, while the mass majority will answer no, there is no such ability.

In contrast, if you asked 100 seasoned Sales Professionals the same question, the majority would answer yes, you can peek qualify...they *know* - because they've done it!

The "*Peek Qualifying*" Cherry Picking strain eats away the cells in the department of the brain that formulates rational thoughts. It eats away the cells in the cognitive department of the Sales Professional's mind that generate thoughts of common sense. In some cases, it seeps deep inside them and influences their internal drive. It consumes their Sales Spirit and greatly reduces their motivation to generate the most sales possible.

> It consumes the Sales Spirit and greatly reduces motivation to generate the maximum Sales possible.

In the worst cases, Sales Professionals have let fully qualified prospects just walk away for no logical reason. I have heard some pretty outrageous reasons.

"Are you kidding? No, I didn't give him a tour. If he is that old and that big I *know* he wouldn't have signed up. Don't worry, it's still early, someone younger and a little smaller will show up and I'll sell them."

Managers have long been puzzled as to why brand-new Sales Professionals do not show symptoms of *peek qualifying*. When brand-new Sales Professionals start working at a new company, they are seen working *every* customer. The *peek qualifiying* strain only affects *seasoned* Sales Professionals. My conclusion is that peek qualifying is passed from the seasoned Sales Professionals to the newbies.

The following story is about the lesson I learned about this particular Cherry Picking strain, because it attacked me. Fortunately, it was a mild case and my immune system was able to fight it. It was clearly a classic example of *peek qualifying*.

In my mid-20s I worked at a large electronics store for a very short time. This store sold all types of TVs, stereos, major appliances, etc. To survive, I had to learn the retail sales game really fast. I was a young rookie, and I was up against some old pros. Some of the old pros in that store had been in the business for 20+ years, but this actually *was* my first rodeo.

Right away, I learned about the store's "bait-and-switch" marketing strategy. The store would advertise an item at cost, or even *below cost,* just to get people to walk in the store. And when they came in, us Super Salesmen would make them believe that they really didn't want that advertised, below-cost item. We did our *complete, planned presentation,* and sold them a better, more expensive unit than the advertised one. We were taught not to bash the advertised item because that would discredit the store. Instead, we would tell them that the advertised model was a good quality model; it just didn't have many features to it. Basically, you could only turn it on and off. It was of good quality; it was just the very basic model.

Right after explaining the simple features of the basic model, we would take the customer to the absolute top of the line model. We would point at the price tag for only one reason: to scare them. We put them into price shock. Rarely did we sell the very top of the line of anything in this store. In fact, as a selling strategy, we sold against it.

This store knew that the "top of the line" sales only represented a very small percentage of total sales, so they taught the Sales Professionals to use it as a means to an end. They knew that the mass majority of people bought in the middle; they did not buy the cheapest item, and they did not buy the most expensive. They bought in the middle. Somewhere along the line in my selling career, I started calling the previous selling strategy "the Three Bears Presentation". You presented too little, too much, and then at last…the one that was just right!

The Sales Professionals in this store had to move a customer to at least one or two models up from the below-cost, advertised item, in order for him or her to earn a "spiff"— in other words, a "commission" on the sale. The advertised item - the "teaser" item - did not pay any spiff or commission. A

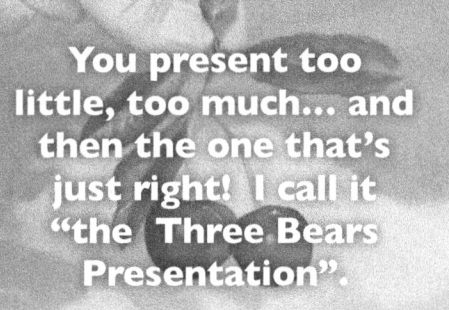

You present too little, too much… and then the one that's just right! I call it "the Three Bears Presentation".

Sales Professional was only paid a volume bonus on that sale of 1% of the purchase price, and <u>that was all</u>.

The store couldn't pay a spiff or commission on the advertised "teaser" item for one simple reason: the teaser item was advertised *at or below the store's cost*. It was not the intention of the store to sell any of them; it was simply a way to get people in the store.

The following exemplifies how the Sales Professional's income would be different by selling the teaser model vs. a move-up model:

Salesperson #1

They simply sell the advertised teaser model; let's say, a refrigerator for $599.00. He or she receives their 1% volume bonus of $5.99. They get no spiff or commission. They make a whopping total of six bucks on this sale. If they continued this behavior for very long, they would have not only starved, but they would have been out of a job.

Salesperson #2

This Sales Professional sells 2 models up from the teaser model. They sell a refrigerator for $749.00. They receive their 1% of the volume which was $7.50, plus they receive a spiff, a commission on this sale of $18.00. So the $7.50 plus the $18.00 commission brings this Sales Professional's total pay to $25.50...over 4 times more than the previous Salesman who just sold the advertised special.

Salesperson #2 was probably the salesperson of the quarter. When the customers come in with the ad and want to see the "advertised special", this Sales Professional does a *complete, planned presentation* every time. They do what I call "the Three Bears Presentation" on *every* customer.

Here is an example of this Super Salesman at work:

After starting at the advertised special, the Sales Professional goes right to the top of the line refrigerator. They go from the $599.00 model to the $2,499.00 model, and they do a complete presentation on it.

After hearing all about the top of the line model for $2,499.00, the customer explains that they would rather spend $2,500.00 on a car for their college student, instead of a refrigerator. The customer gracefully bows out and nicely explains that "they probably would not use all of those fancy features" on that top of the line model.

Of course the Sales Professional has seen people object to buying the top of the line before. This is *not* the Sales Professional's first rodeo. From the Sales Professional's view, the strategy of slapping the customer with sticker shock worked perfectly.

After pretending to show some empathy, the Super Salesman pauses for a moment and snaps their fingers. Their eyes open wide, and they look as if some divine revelation had just enlightened them. They take the customer down to the $749.00 model fridge.

The Sales Professional does a complete, planned presentation on it. They mention that it has *exactly the same* internal parts as the $2,499.00 model. They share their revelation that it's really the same as the other one; it just "did not have those fancy features" that the customer "wouldn't use anyway."

The people buy it hook, line and sinker.

But wait...that's not all. This Super Salesman sells them the extended warranty and gets another $20.00, raising his or her grand total payout from $25.50 to $45.50. The end result for them is now $45 vs. the other Salesman's six bucks!

Sales Professionals that perform a complete, planned presentation receive much bigger paychecks.

That's quite a different paycheck for Super Salesman #2... not to mention the job security.

All of the previous information leads to the following lesson that I learned early in my sales career. I was so blessed by this. Again, learning from this experience early in my career added a huge amount to my earnings.

I had worked at this super electronics store for about a week or so, and I had already learned quite a bit. One thing that really surprised me was the way the salespeople worked the flow of incoming customers. There was no "alternating up" system; there was no keeping track of who got which customers. It was simply a free-for-all. I guess if you were really greedy, you could wait at the door and catch people right as they walked in the store.

I tried that.

I was quickly and sharply informed by the store manager that this was not a good idea. He warned me that he could not guarantee my safety in the parking lot after work. After a few days, I found that working the traffic in a free-for-all system just seemed to work itself out. The Sales Professionals had their favorite things they liked to sell. For example, "Old Man Fred" liked the refrigerators and freezers. He just hung out there. He was a seasoned veteran and he claimed his territory.

I stayed out of "Fred's Land".

Some people just hung around certain places in the store, and then there were a few like me: we were roamers, we roamed around. I liked to be all over the store – except, of course, "Fred's Land". When the customers walked in, there was never a fistfight over them. Every now and then, a pretty female customer would come in and you would see her get swarmed. But the rule was simple: whoever greeted her first had rights. It was a funny thing to watch sometimes.

This is the part of the story I want you to get. You have an opportunity to really learn from this.

One day, I noticed two very young men walk in. They looked to be in their teens, and they were purple. You can assign whatever color you choose; I choose "purple". One of them had a newspaper in his hand.

All of the seasoned Sales Professionals with experience quickly *peeked* at him and they automatically *knew* that the young, purple man was looking for an advertised special, a teaser item. You know, one of those no-spiff-paying things. Based entirely on their *peek qualifying*, the seasoned Sales Professionals just *knew* that these two young, purple guys could only buy something cheap, because after all, just look at them.

> **Based entirely on "peek qualifying", the seasoned Sales Professionals just "knew" that's all he could afford; after all - just *look* at him.**

Sure enough, the two young purple guys walked over to the microwaves. The kid with the paper walked right up to the below-cost, teaser unit. That microwave was like $99.00. The young men stood there for a while, opening the microwave and reading the bullet card that listed the features it had. They looked around the store, looking to see if someone would come help them.

No one would.

I looked around the store as well, and I saw the seasoned Sales Professionals *peek* at the young, purple guys, and then quickly look away as if they had not seen them. The seasoned Sales Professionals just *knew* that it was only going to be a $99.00 sale that paid no spiff. In other words, the seasoned Sales Professionals did not want to help him and only make the 1% of the sale, which was only going to be 99 cents. They simply refused.

I am no hero. It's quite the contrary. I felt something coming on, like when you think you might be coming down with something – but you don't. Somehow, your body just fights it and you don't get sick. Perhaps I was catching the *peek qualifying* strain of Cherry Picking from the seasoned, Sales Professionals, because I wanted to help this young man, but a little voice in my head said don't.

I wanted to fit in with my peers. I wanted to be one of the "Sales Gang". However, rather than join the rest of the gang and not help the young man, I thought that *any* money was better than *no* money. So I thought that I would walk up to these young, purple guys, write the deal in seconds, and get my 99 cents in literally less than a minute. My attitude was that I was going to make an extra buck here in less than a minute, and it would be easy and painless.

I walked up to the two young, purple guys and introduced myself. The young man with the paper asked, "Can you tell me about this microwave?"

"Sure," I eagerly replied. "It's great," I added with enthusiasm. I did a quick demonstration and said that it was a great model for the money. I asked him if he wanted to buy it as I got out a ticket to write it up. I skipped "the Three Bears" complete, planned presentation. I did not take him to the top of the line and back to the middle of the line because…well, just *look* at him. He was a young, purple teenager in jeans and a T-shirt, and I just *knew* that he couldn't afford anything else. As I was thinking this, I felt something going on in my head; things were getting a little fuzzy.

The young man looked puzzled. He walked over to a microwave that was $150.00 and asked, "What does this one do?"

I quickly explained that it just had different power levels and that was all. I explained that the basic model he originally looked at had one power level, "On", and that the more expensive one had many different power levels. I was quick to discount the extra power levels as any real advantage and explained that most people would only use the one power level anyway.

I further explained that the public simply thinks that "more is better", so manufacturers take advantage of that thinking. They add extra features to their models and people buy them, and yet people never use all of those extra features. I assured the young man that the basic model would work out just fine for him and I asked him to buy it again – because just look at him – that's all he could afford.

He still looked puzzled. He walked over to an even more expensive microwave. He asked, "What does this one do?"

This is where I started to lose it. I *knew* this was why all the seasoned Sales Professionals did not approach this guy. The old pros just *knew*, because they had the experience and I didn't. I thought, "This was my lesson." This young man was now going to take up my time. And while I was wasting my time with this guy, who was probably going to end up with the $99.00 microwave anyway, the old pros would land the customers that would buy a much bigger ticket item. I just *knew* it.

At this point in time, I thought that all of the old pros in the store were all snickering at me in their minds, thinking, "Welcome to the business, rookie!"

I thought to myself that it was only going to take this once; I was going to learn fast. I *knew* what I would do next time.

Hindsight is 20-20. This is where I caught Cherry Picking... from the seasoned Sales Professionals.

Of course, hindsight is 20-20. Looking back, this was probably where I was catching Cherry Picking from the seasoned Sales Professionals. But for some reason, unknown to me to this day, my body was fighting it.

As I saw the young man looking puzzled at the more expensive microwave, I kicked into another gear...I did my job. I did what they hired me to do; make a complete, *planned presentation*, and sell their merchandise. After all, that's what they were paying me for.

I did the complete "Three Bears" presentation – just like they trained me.

Guess what? The young, purple man bought a middle model. It was around $150.00…and it paid a spiff! I was euphoric! The total ticket was going to pay me about $5.00, and it took less than 10 minutes. Not bad.

But it was not over. The young man then asked me about TV sets; he wanted to know where the TV sets were. As I said, "Follow me," the Cherry Picking virus in my brain was beginning to overtake me. It was kidnapping my reality thought, "Make a big commission," and in its place was sending me the thought, "You are wasting your time. Just look at him – he can't afford it." I could not stop that little voice in my head.

The young man followed me as I lead him to the TVs. Of course, I was taking him to the cheap, portable TV section, where the little 13" TVs were. Why? Well, just look at him, that's all that he could afford, right? That's what I heard from the little voice inside my head.

> **Well, just *look* at him, that's all he can afford, right? That's what I heard from the little voice inside *my head*.**

He stopped me midway through the store. He wanted the big console TV, the kind that sat on the ground. (This tells you how long ago this was. I said I learned this lesson *early* in my career.) I took him to the console TV section, and as he looked at the TVs with a puzzled look, it hit me hard. I *was* right.

This really was too good to be true. The whole thing about writing the microwave in just a few minutes and earning a quick commission, well, that just wasn't the way this was going to turn out. I *knew* I was going to get burned. Not only that, I was going to be the joke of the day at this store.

Oh well, I did what they trained me to do anyway. I made a complete, *planned presentation*. I even kicked into gear and lead him through a bunch of sets and landed him on a particular manufacturer that I will not name. That particular manufacturer at the time was paying the highest spiff of all. It paid more than any other manufacturer. (I found out later that this is why about 1 in 3 households had one.) After I interacted with the young man and performed a knock-it-out-of-the-park, complete, planned presentation, I asked him to buy it; I closed.

But as I was asking him to buy it, the little voice in my head was saying that this was just really all for practice. The TV I was asking him to buy is $800.00. With his micro at $150.00 and now this TV, we were at $1,000.00. Inside my head the little voice was telling me that this young man was going to say, "Thanks, but I am just looking right now. I will definitely keep it in mind."

And when I asked him to buy it, guess what?

He said, "I'll take it."

Right after he said he would take it he asked, "Where are the stereos? I want to get a stereo too."

Now I was totally confused. I was feeling a little dizzy. The Cherry Picking thoughts and my reality thoughts were at war. I was feeling lightheaded as I asked him to follow me to the stereo department.

On our way to the stereo department the young man saw a huge display in the middle of the store. It was set up as a wall unit. It had a monitor TV, a stereo system complete with dual cassette player, and a top of the line Hi-Fi VCR. (Remember, I said this happened early in my career.) When the young, purple man first saw the wall unit display his jaw dropped and his eyes got big. He asked questions and I answered them. We interacted well because we were in rapport. The short story: I did what they paid me to do; I made a *complete, planned presentation*.

He said, "I should just get this. It has everything."

It was $2,299.00…before tax.

He asked for his friend's opinion, who had remained silent throughout. His friend gave him the nod.

And then it hit me hard. Instead of the reality thought, "You just earned yourself a big commission," the Cherry Picking thought was, "He is now going to ask for financing, and of course he doesn't qualify – because after all, just look at him." I thought that I just went from the joke of the day to the joke of the week. I noticed that I had attracted an audience. When I was in full demonstration at the wall unit and was asking for the sale, some old pros were looking on. I sure liked them watching me then, but I did not like them watching me now.

Sure enough, the young purple man asked, "Have you got financing?"

Like a slow leak in a big balloon in polyester, I started to deflate. I answered, "We do." I asked him to go over to a table and sit down. Now I needed to continue doing my job, just like they trained me to do. I now had to make a complete, *planned presentation* on <u>all</u> of the extended warranties on <u>each and every item</u> on his ticket.

His ticket had about 5 or 6 separate items. Each individual item needed a complete presentation, and each extended warranty presentation was going to take about 5 minutes. I just *knew* that I was now badly burned for quite some time. But again, I kicked into gear and did my job. I did what they hired me to do; I made a complete, planned presentation on the extended warranty of each one of the items on his ticket.

He bought them all, except one. Ironically, he did not buy the extended warranty on the microwave.

I added up his ticket; it was around $2,800.00. He then asked again, "Have you got financing?"

I began to feel faint as I answered, "Yes, we have financing, and I will take you back there and introduce you to the financing people." But I felt compelled to help this young man. I wanted to explain to him about the financing and how the qualifying worked. This was no longer a quick "*peek qualifying*" thought because by now, I had spent 30-40 minutes with him.

The simple fact was that he was a very young man and that he needed a job with verifiable income in order to qualify for the financing. And after all – I had spent 30–40 minutes with him – long enough to *know for sure* that he could not qualify. That's what the little voice in my head was saying.

I explained to him how the financing process worked. I explained that he would need to fill out an application and that they would run his credit. I asked him if he had any credit. He said no. I asked him if he had a job. He explained that he worked for his mother.

Light bulbs went off in my head…Mom could possibly help.

I asked him, "What do you do for your mother?"

He answered, "I clean her apartments. When somebody moves out, I clean the apartments."

I asked, "Do you get a pay stub that shows your hours and your pay?"

He answered, "No, she just pays me cash."

My heart sunk. I looked around the store to see how many onlookers there were. I wondered how many of the seasoned old pros were getting an instant laugh, and how many would laugh about it later.

At this time, Cherry Picking thoughts were claiming victory in my head. I thought that the seasoned Sales Professionals all *knew* better. They did not help this young, purple man because they were experienced *peek* qualifiers.

> I actually believed that the old pros had perfected their "peek qualifying" ability, and because I didn't have that skill yet, I was now getting burned.

The old pros had perfected their "*peek qualifying*" ability, and because I was brand-new and didn't have that skill, I was now getting burned.

In a friendly and somber manner, I explained to the young man, "The finance company would have to verify your income. Without proof of income, you would not qualify."

The young, purple man was quick to inform me, "They can call my mother. She will tell them what she pays me."

I overheard someone snicker.

With empathy I informed the young man that the finance company would not allow that. I explained to him that all verifications had to be confirmed on paper. I further explained that people could just make up whatever story they wanted to and have their friends or family just verify it by phone, and so the finance company would not do that. I was letting him down easy because I had rapport with him and I was genuinely interested in helping him.

As I did another quick scan around the store for seasoned Sales Professionals that might be enjoying the view of my crash and burn, the young man mumbled something to his friend. I heard his friend answer, "A couple of hundred."

The young man reached into his pocket and pulled out a thick wad of money. As he counted it, I saw that it was all one hundred dollar bills. He counted his wad and asked his friend for his couple of hundred.

"I'll just pay cash," the young, purple man said.

It was all there, all $2,800.00...in cash. In fact, he needed some change. I took him up to the cashier and made sure that he was taken care of. He thanked me on his way out. I felt as if a new friend was leaving the store, and perhaps we would see each other again someday.

I now did one more scan of the store. I knew that most of the old pros saw it all, but they would just *"peek"* at me, and then quickly turn away.

My head was clearing up. That little voice was gone. I felt some positive energy that was uplifting. I felt good.

I was so blessed for the previous experience to have happened so early in my sales career. I firmly believe that the lesson I learned from it allowed me to move up a level or two in lifestyle. By recognizing when the Cherry Picking Virus hit me at various times in my selling career, and by fighting it off, my income level throughout my career was higher.

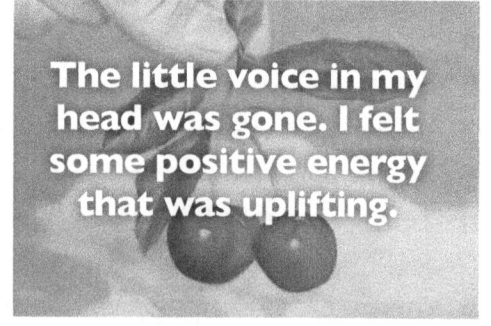

The little voice in my head was gone. I felt some positive energy that was uplifting.

In hindsight, I was extremely fortunate to have that personal experience because there were no books like this one to learn about this.

To see how much this type of Cherry Picking may be costing you, fill out the following chart, counting the number of your Cherry Picks in which you chose to <u>not</u> perform your *complete, planned presentation.*

In The Last 12 Months

_____ Cherry Picks due to a person looking like they did not qualify based on what they were wearing.

_____ Cherry Picks due to the car the person drove.

_____ Cherry Picks due to the house they lived in

_____ Cherry Picks due to some other visual reason and you just *knew* that they would not buy.

_____ Total Cherry Picks

X _____ Average Commission

= _____ Total Income Loss for 12 Months

In the next chapter, you will learn of yet another type of Cherry Picking.

Chapter Highlights

- It is believed that brand-new Sales Professionals enter a company Cherry Picking-Free, and learn to Cherry Pick from the seasoned Sales Professionals.

- The "Peek Qualifying " strain affects a Sales Professional's visual and cognitive processes.

- Based on a quick "peek", seasoned Sales Professionals claim they "know" if a person is going to buy.

- As a result of Cherry Picking, a Sales Professional must live one or two lifestyles down due to their loss of income.

FOUR

Virus #2 Type "Enne"

This sister virus appears to be costing Sales Professionals the most. It is very challenging to track this type of Cherry Picking virus, due to the nature of its attack. The simple fact is that the mass majority of Sales Professionals are unaware of its attack. This Cherry Picking strain affects *all* Sales Professionals selling *every* product and *every* service.

Similar to the *Peek Qualifying* strain, this Cherry Picking strain also affects the Sales Professional's thoughts. But instead of affecting vision and reality thoughts about different people and how they look, this wicked virus affects the Sales Professional's reality thoughts and generates numerous *silly* excuses for choosing *not* to perform a complete, planned presentation.

Here's how this virus strain works:

The Sales Professional greets a customer, and during the greeting, in the Sales Professional's mind, a reality thought is generated that says, "I need to perform my complete sales presentation - because this is a potential sale." After all, that is reality. But this Cherry Picking virus kidnaps that reality thought, "potential sale," and it its place the virus sends a prank thought like, "I don't want to do a complete presentation right now because _____." Fill in the blank with a silly reason like "It's almost time to go to lunch."

Over the years, this nasty virus has multiplied and run wild. I see countless Sales Professionals in all professions now victim to this overabundance of silly reasons that they actually believe are justified reasons to <u>not</u> perform a complete, planned presentation on a customer.

This Cherry Picking strain has been named the "Enne ol Reezon" strain.

Examples of some of the silly reasons that this strain generates include but are not limited to:

- It's almost lunch time

- It's just after lunch time

- It's too early; I just got here

- It's kind of late; I was just about to leave

- I just sold one; I have to turn in my paperwork

- I already have enough deals for the week

- I already have enough deals for the month

- I already have enough deals for the quarter

- I already have enough deals to win the contest

- I have enough deals right now

- I just got into a fight with my _____ and I'm not in a good mood

- My boss is out of town

- My boss will be by soon and I have to talk to him or her

- Somebody called and said they would be here an hour ago, and I am waiting for them

- I was making follow-up calls

- I needed to check on my kids

- It doesn't matter; just make it up

Thank goodness that this type of Cherry Picking does not affect our emergency rescue workers. How horrible would it be if rescue workers Cherry Picked?

Thank goodness that this type of Cherry Picking does not affect our emergency crew workers.

Imagine this: A Sales Professional hears that a heavy rain storm might be headed their way. So they Cherry Pick and cut their last presentation of the day short; after all, they heard a bad storm might come their way.

On the way home, they stop at an intersection. The water rises so fast that their car stalls. They get up on the roof of their car and call for help. The rescue crew gets there fast and sets up the rescue.

One of the rescue workers gets tied off from the shore. He starts walking across the rising water to rescue the Sales Professional standing on the roof of their car. The water is still rising fast. As the rescue worker reaches the car, he slows down his rescue attempt and haphazardly goes through the motions. He then stops the rescue attempt and goes back to shore.

The Sales Professional is swept away and drowns.

The supervisor on the scene runs over to the rescue worker and asks him, "What happened out there?" The man answers, "I want to go to lunch. Don't worry, it's still *early* in the storm; I just *know* that there will be another victim and I'll rescue them for sure!"

"I had to cut it short. It's my nephew's birthday and the family is getting together for dinner."

As you can see, Cherry Picking would be very costly if it attacked our rescue workers or emergency room workers. People might die. In sales performance, as opposed to costing lives, Cherry Picking costs *lifestyles*. Sales Professionals are forced to move down a level or two in their lifestyle because of their lower income that results from Cherry Picking.

"Cherry Pickers"

We all learn though our own life experiences. Some people are gifted with an open-minded approach to life. The gifted ones with an open mind can learn by listening to the experiences of others. They learn by listening to the triumphs and defeats that other people experience. You can save yourself the pain of going through some of the same failures that other people have experienced, as well as reap the benefits of modeling successful people.

Unfortunately, some people are just stubborn and close-minded. It is a common flaw of being human. When some people hear about a mistake that someone else made, they believe that if they were to do the <u>exact same thing</u>, the outcome would be different for them, because they are *different*. Unfortunately, those close-minded people suffer a bumpy ride through life. Another way at looking at this is by calling this the "I already know" syndrome.

Unfortunately, close-minded people experience a bumpy ride though life.

You can easily recognize the "I already know" syndrome when you start to explain something to someone and they say "I know" before you are finished talking. In fact, some people repeat the phrase "I know" throughout their daily common dialogue. This closed-mindedness blocks that individual's growth. This closed-mindedness limits an individual's acquisition of knowledge. I believe that you are what you say you are – you are your word. With this insight, you can see that if an individual walks through life with an "I know" view, their acquiring knowledge would be blocked. This view is in the same realm as Cherry Picking.

In the next chapter, you will learn about what fuels Cherry Picking thoughts. When you learn more about the cause, you will gain invaluable insight on how to recognize it and see how it affects you. By learning and applying this knowledge, you will have the opportunity to move up a lifestyle or two as a result of your increase in income.

But first, take a moment and fill out the following chart, and estimate the amount of income you lost last year due to Cherry Picking thoughts.

In the Last 12 Months

I Cherry Picked and did not do a complete, planned presentation because:

____ It was my first presentation of the day and I was not ready yet

____ I was just about to go to lunch

____ I just got back from lunch

____ I was just about to go home

____ I wasn't in the right mood

____ I was in the middle of something else

____ I just sold one

____ I already sold enough today

____ I sold enough this week

____ I sold enough for the month

____ I already won the sales contest

____ My boss is out of town

____ My boss just yelled at me to sell something and he shook me up

____ The price, product or service is about to change; I am just wasting my time selling this now.

____ I am thinking about getting another job because I am just not selling enough here.

____ Whatever other silly reason I felt was justified at the time

_____ Total Cherry Picks

X _____ My average commission

_____ Total income lost in last 12 months

Now, add together the previous losses from "*Peek Qualifying*" with the losses of "*Enne ol Reezon*".

_____ Losses from the *Peek Qualifying* strain

+

_____ Losses from the *Enne 'ol Reezon* strain

=

_____ Grand total Cherry Picking losses in last 12 months

In science and medicine, you have to identify the cause before you can find a cure. In the next chapter, you will learn what causes Cherry Picking. You will be astounded.

Chapter Highlights

- The "Enne ol Reezon" strain affects a Sales Professional's reality thoughts.

- Thank goodness that our emergency crew workers are not affected by Cherry Picking.

- There seems to be a growing list of silly reasons why people Cherry Pick.

- The losses due to Cherry Picking are staggering.

- How much does Cherry Picking cost you?

FIVE

The Cause

s you have seen, Cherry Picking is very costly. It is running wild and out of control. Vast resources have been invested in researching the true cause of Cherry Picking, and the good news is that we have found it.

Brain neurologists are still researching the vast web of neurons in the brain to pinpoint *exactly* where in the brain thoughts of Cherry Picking are ignited, but what they have found so far is rather austere.

In all Sales scenarios — from low-ticket Retail Sales to big-ticket Real Estate Sales — in *every* Sales game there is what is called a "conversion formula". That conversion formula says that you are going to sell one **The well known conversion formula says that you will sell one in X number of units of traffic.** in X number of units of traffic. In other words, you will close the deal on one in X number of prospects that you meet and make a presentation to.

Whatever industry that you are in, whatever product or service that you sell, your management has been exposed to numbers from research firms that spell out what the average conversion rate is in your industry. I have the numbers from the Home Building Industry and the Property Management Industry because I have spent over a decade providing specialized training in those respected industries.

I have viewed thousands of hours of single-family and multi-family video shops. I have walked through the front door of thousands of model homes all across North America and watched Sales Professionals work me. That incredible opportunity afforded me the unique and invaluable experience of evaluating several thousand Sales Presentations on a national level. I contrasted my evaluations with my previous 20 years of selling big-tickets, as well as reflecting on the extensive Sales Training that I experienced throughout my selling career.

For many years, I traveled 3 and 4 weeks out of the month, evaluating Sales Presentations across North America. Although I observed some slight variables in local cultures (folks in Salt Lake City were a little different than the folks in Miami), I found an overwhelming common denominator in all of the Sales Professionals that I encountered. I will not say that all Sales People are the same, because that is definitely not true. However, all Sales Professional are human, and there is a basic, human nature that affects all Sales Professionals.

As you read these next few paragraphs, keep in mind this thought: People can make simple things complicated. It is human nature to take a relatively simple thing and beat it to death.

Perhaps you have experienced an issue in your past, either personal or professional, and you were confused about how to handle it because you had so many different thoughts about it. You thought about it as you drove in your car; you thought about it in the shower; it could have been your last thought at night and your first thought in the morning. You struggled on deciding which way to go. But afterwards, when it was all settled, you thought to yourself, "That was easy...that really didn't need to be so complicated."

The true cause of Cherry Picking is really pretty simple.

Consider this: if you were told, like the Sales Professionals in the Home Building Industry are told, that you were going to sell to an average of 1 in 20 people that walk through the door, wouldn't it be human nature for you to wonder when "*the one*" that was going to buy was going to show up?

> **If your marketing department told you what your customer profile was, wouldn't it be human nature to be "looking" for them?**

Furthermore, as a Sales Professional, you are exposed to information such as your "Average Customer Profile". You are savvy to whom your company is marketing and have a mental picture of whom they would like to have walk through your door. Your company has set your expectations of who you will probably sell to, so you develop your mental picture of what they would look like.

On any given day, it would simply be human nature to guess if the very next person was the one in X, or if they were coming tomorrow or the next day. You couldn't help but wonder not only on what day "the one" would show up, but also be looking for that mental picture you manufactured of "the one" to show up.

It would then simply be human nature to quickly measure up every customer that you meet and quickly match him or her up to your "expected customer profile"... the one that you manufactured in your mind. Clearly, the major flaw in this is that every Sales Professional manufactures a slightly different mental picture of the expected customer profile.

In reality, it is quite common for most seasoned Sales Professionals to command control of when and to whom they are going to sell. The fact is, seasoned Sales Professionals choose their "A Game" days. Another simple fact is that it is very common for seasoned Sales Professionals to prefer to sell to people that they like and people they would want to work with. Can you blame them? You can blame them, and you need to, but at the same time, keep in mind that Sales Professionals are only human.

Compare the following charts. See how they correlate.

THE CAUSE

Sales Presentation Scores

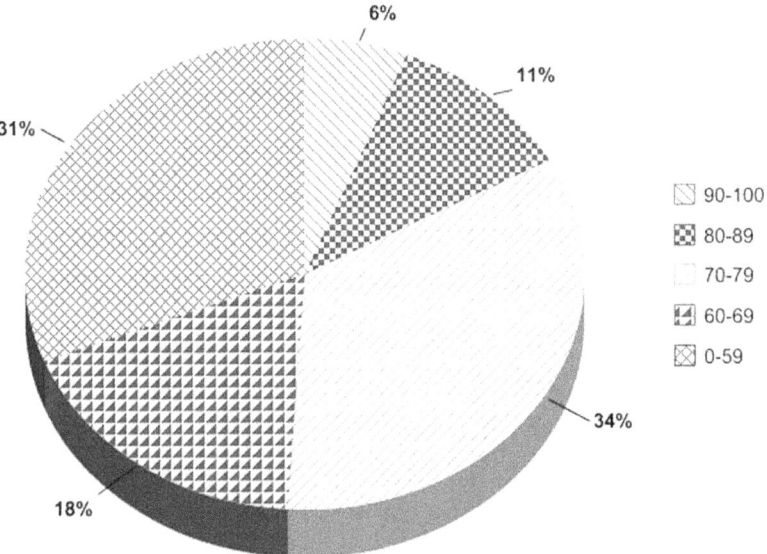

6%
11%
31%
34%
18%

90-100
80-89
70-79
60-69
0-59

Progressive Insights

Sales Professional's Customer Preference Level

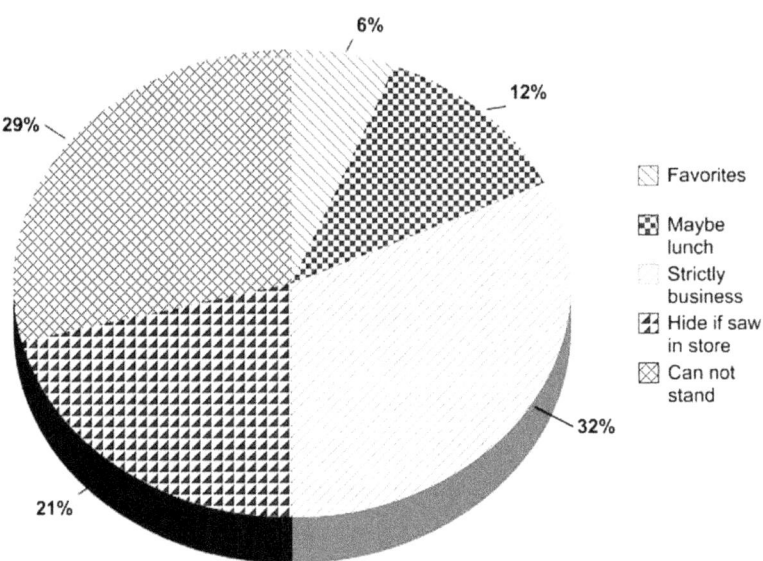

6%
12%
29%
32%
21%

Favorites
Maybe lunch
Strictly business
Hide if saw in store
Can not stand

Progressive Insights

As you can see, the charts show that Sales Professionals make their best presentations to the people "they want to sell to". In other words, the lower the customer preference level, the lower the presentation score.

A good question to ask is, "Where were the one in X's?" How many one in X's were actually at the lower end of the "customer preference level"? In real life selling, the real one in X, the real buyer, might receive the worst presentation.

I believe that you cannot hold someone accountable for doing something wrong without first providing him or her with the knowledge of how to do it right. Once you have set proper expectations, I believe that you then receive an agreement from the team member that they accept those expectations. Lastly, you receive a commitment from the team member that they will meet your expectations. Only then can you "Inspect the Expect".

A common flaw that I have found in many companies is that they critique the less-than-expected results from their Sales Professionals without not only providing sufficient training but also without receiving proper commitments from the Sales Professionals.

In my company, the commitments I find common with Sales Professionals and Managers is that they will "sell all they can." The sales goals are made up and the Sales Professionals are asked to commit to them. But simply being committed to a sales goal of X a month or X for the year without proper, strategic planning and practice, would be like a sports team saying they are committed to winning the championship, but not outlining their strategy and practicing it.

Winning is not a strategy – it is a desired end result of the strategy you implemented. I help companies make that distinction.

Sales results are most pleasurable when all team members "buy in" to the company's selling strategy and selling system. A common mistake is for a company to leave it with their Sales Professionals to "sell all you can", supported by no strategy or system.

I could start another book here about companies that excelled from their commitment to their strategy, but I want to go back to the previously mentioned conversion rates and customer profiles. Although there are some rewards in understanding conversion rates and customer profiles, there also is a risk of that information backfiring and being misused.

For example, it could be shortly after their last sale, perhaps too soon for them to think that the next one in X buyer has shown up, when the Sales Professional meets a person that does not quite look like the exact customer profile – the one they manufactured in their mind. It would be human nature for the Sales Professional to decide, "They are not *the one*." As a result, the Sales Professional performs a horrific Sales presentation and kills the sale — and feels justified in doing so — because after all, since that customer didn't buy, the Sales Professional believes it was quite obvious that they were not *the one*.

On the other hand, sales could be down, so the Sales Professional could say to themselves, "I have to sell one today!" And in having such thoughts about their own personal needs to make a sale, the Sales Professional could "Cherry Pick" the very next person that matches the alleged customer profile, the one that they have manufactured in their mind, and try really hard to sell them. However, this particular customer is not ready to buy today. But the Sales Professional Cherry Picks this customer and wants to make them *the one*, so the Sales Professional applies undue pressure and hard closes the customer out of context. Things really get screwed up!

A customer that could have been the one *tomorrow*, will *never* be the one after the way they were just treated.

After evaluating thousands of Sales Presentations on a national level, I found certain relationships between Sales Presentations where the sale was not asked for vs. Sales Presentations where the Sales Professional did close and did ask for the sale. Again, as I mentioned earlier, it is human nature to want to take a simple issue and beat it to death. Compare the charts following, and see what jumps out at you.

THE CAUSE

Sales Presentation Scores

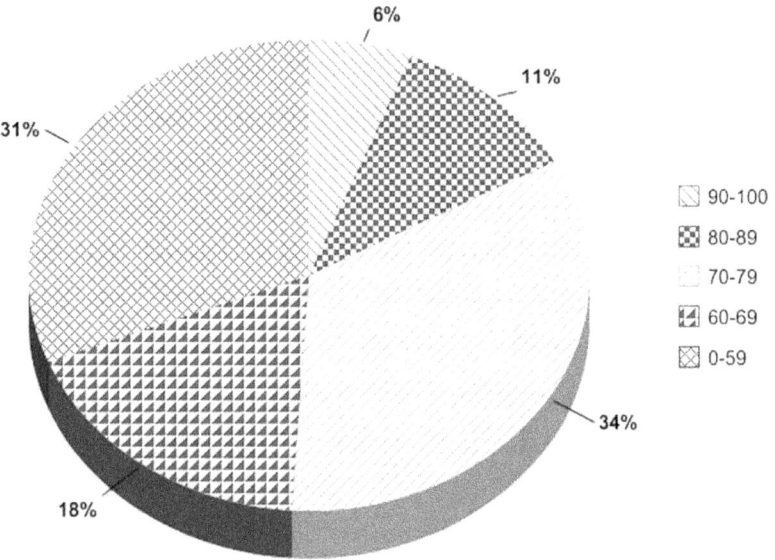

6%
11%
31%
34%
18%

90-100
80-89
70-79
60-69
0-59

Progressive Insights

Post Presentation, Customer Asked "Would You Buy?"

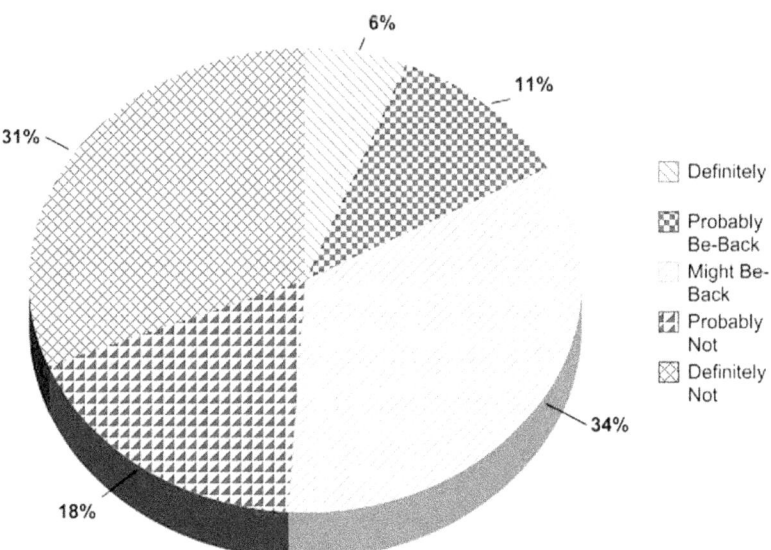

6%
11%
31%
34%
18%

Definitely
Probably Be-Back
Might Be-Back
Probably Not
Definitely Not

Progressive Insights

Evaluating all of the previous charts made it very clear to me that the sale...the closing of the deal...relied heavily on the Sales Professional's desire and work ethic. Imagine that.

In my opinion, the real profile that you want to sell to is the person who will be able to pay you; you want to sell to *every* customer whose check you can cash. It doesn't matter if their check has flowers on it, or if it looks too business-like for your taste, or if it has Mickey Mouse on it; the only thing that matters... is that you can cash their check!

I have to practice this concept in my own company, because in my business I deal with people in sales and operational management. As you know, some of those folks are wackos; they're clueless. But this isn't E-Harmony; we don't have to be compatible in 114 different dimensions in order to do business with each other.

In my view, I need to deliver to my clients a better-perceived value than my competitors and then cash my client's checks, even the Mickey Mouse ones.

Don't misunderstand me — I believe that great business relationships are paramount, and they directly dictate the overall success of the client-vendor business.

Now, if the Cherry Picking thoughts on when and to whom you would make a complete, planned presentation were all that you had to deal with, I would think that you could overcome those Cherry Picking thoughts. You would tell yourself that you were simply going to treat *every* person that you made a presentation to as if they were "*the one*". You could easily own the idea that every customer deserves your complete "A Game" presentation.

You could say to yourself everyday that you were going to perform what I call "The Alphabet Presentation", and sing the entire alphabet with your customer. From A-Z, you would sing the whole song with every customer – unless, of course, somewhere along the way the customer stopped you.

Whatever product or service you are selling, if you approached every Sales Presentation with the idea that you were going to sing the alphabet with every customer until they stopped you, you would generate more sales.

But you don't operate that way, and I will help you with why you don't.

Clearly, you agree that it is simply human nature for Sales Professionals to Cherry Pick; to simply choose when and to whom they are going to perform their complete "A Game" presentation. Some Sales Professionals have lived a Cherry Picking lifestyle for so long that it has become a bad work ethic and bad habit for them. They forgot when they were new and sold Cherry Picking-free. For them to take action to eliminate Cherry Picking will not be easy. Any and all habits are a challenge to change; that is simply human nature.

However, as if the previously-mentioned Cherry Picking thoughts alone were not a big enough challenge for you to deal with… there is yet another hurdle that you have to jump.

Consider for a moment that the original thought of Cherry Picking by itself is just a small flame – like that of a small cigarette lighter. Alone, the small flame can be blown out without much effort. However, if that small flame were to touch something like a stack of dried hay doused with lighter fluid, the fire would mushroom quickly out of control.

The point is that there is a highly combustible fuel in your mind that fuels your small, petty thoughts of Cherry Picking. What starts out as a petty thought like, "They seem a little out of our profile," or a petty thought like, "I am not sure I really like their personality," or "I was about to go to lunch," eventually explodes into thoughts like, "I am not going to make a complete presentation to them because_____ _____ (fill in any reason)."

The highly combustible fuel that fuels your Cherry Picking thoughts is your EGO.

Every human being has an ego; it is simply a matter of to what degree. The ego develops at an early age and grows with each individual at different rates. Some people hide their ego well, while others seem to be victims of their ego; they display it daily for everyone to notice. Their ego bullies their intellect, and subdues their rational thinking.

Researchers are studying why certain groups of people have uncontrollable egos. One group where huge egos have been found is serial killers. These unfortunate people lose their perception of reality and lose control to their egos. Their strong egos fuel their thoughts in such a convincing manner that they perform horrific crimes. They actually believe that what they are doing at the time is "justified".

Sales Professionals also feel that they are "justified" when they perform horrific presentations - and kill a sale.

I find it incredible that our ego can actually alter our rational thinking. Yet little to no classes on how to identify our ego and keep it in check are offered in our high schools or universities.

The ego influences a Sales Professional's thoughts about when and to whom they wish to sell to, and their ego toys with their intellect by using past thoughts against them that are deeply anchored in their minds. You see, throughout

The ego toys with a Sales Professional's intellect.

our childhood, we found ways to identify differences in others. Our ego showed us how to draw a line and say that *our* way was the *right* way, and *their* way was *wrong*.

Children do not learn this from their parents…or do they?

Parents may not call anyone something childish like "fatso" in front of their children; instead, they may label an individual or group in a "grown-up" way. For example, they may call a political party "liars and crooks". Or they may have called a particular politician an "idiot". It is common for parents to subject their children to a common thought process like "I am different from them…I am *right* and they are *wrong*."

Almost all adults are challenged with controlling their egos, and unfortunately, most don't. Children see their parents separate themselves from other people in different "grown-up" ways, and children in turn follow that same pattern.

Research has shown that preschool children, from ages 2 – 4, show no resentment towards their fellow preschoolers. This supports the current belief that the desire to separate yourself from all other people is not in your DNA; instead, it is something learned. Our ego tutors us as we grow up into a competitive world.

Understand that <u>resentment</u> is one of the main emotions that power the ego. Millions of people have been killed throughout man's history as a result of the ego working through the emotion of resentment. Often times, emotional resentment could have been over nothing tangible or physical; just a simple belief about something, even something that could not be proven.

An example of a simple belief that no one could prove to be true might be a particular religious belief. The ego says "My belief is right, yours is wrong," and throughout man's history, based on unproven theories, one group slaughtered another.

With many Sales Professionals, it is the ego that quickly ignites their Cherry Picking thoughts to an "Out-of-Reality" level. The ego bullies the Sales Professional's intellect, consumes all of the rational thoughts in their brain, and dictates the inexcusable action of performing a less-than-expected Sales Presentation.

The fuel that the ego uses is to simply identify some kind of *difference* about the customer. The ego convinces you that because they are *different* than what you want them to be, they are inferior. This translates into a Sales Professional's choice on to whom and when to make a complete presentation. When the mind labels a customer as different or less desirable to work with, for any reason manufactured, the Sales Professional transforms this thought to, "I *know* they are not *the one.*"

The reason why I mention all of this is so that you can see the devastating power of the ego. Again, there are very few classes on the ego in our high schools and universities. With no formal education available on the ego, it is simply that Sales Professionals just don't know what they just don't know. You can blame them, but keep in mind, they are only human.

The ego has devastating power, and unfortunately there are little to no classes in our formal education system about the ego.

It appears that there is a current movement for man to recognize the devastation caused by his dominating ego. Some eye-opening revelations have recently been discovered. I highly recommend reading all of Ekhart Tolle's books. I found his writings educational and inspiring.

I find it fascinating that according to Tolle, an individual's ego does not always have to make the individual feel "*superior*" to someone else. A person complaining that they are "*inferior*" for any reason makes the ego smile just as well. The ego doesn't care which it is, as long as the individual feels separated and different. I see examples of this everywhere.

For example, a woman might complain that she did not get a promotion because her breast size was too small, or that she was too old. Her ego is making her feel *inferior* and *different*. It is the ego at work that is the little voice in her head making her say to herself, "I *know* the *real reason* why I didn't get the job."

Another example would be a man that may tell himself that he did not get the promotion because he does not golf very well and does not play with the guys at work. He believed that he was qualified for the job, but his ego made him think he just *knew* that the *real reason* he did not get promoted was that he did not play golf very well. Both of the previous mental conclusions are perfect examples of successful work done by the ego, making people believe that they are *inferior.*

The point is that the ego loves, *"I am the Greatest!"* just as much as, *"Poor Me."* Either way, it makes no difference to the ego. Simply the thought of separation, *"I am different from them,"* and, *"I am right,"* is the objective of the ego. This corresponds with the "I know" syndrome I mentioned earlier. The ego is also a control freak. When the ego fuels Cherry Picking thoughts, the Sales Professional stands little chance to sell in reality. This results in an enormous loss of sales. Performing a poor sales presentation, or even worse, performing no presentation at all, results in little to no net sales.

"They pay me to perform a complete, planned presentation to everyone," is <u>reality</u>. Instead, Sales Professionals lose out to silly reasons, each of which is <u>out of reality</u>. They make choices based on unreal reasons to <u>not</u> perform a complete presentation. An example of being out of reality is, "They were orange people. I work well with blues, but I match up best with greens."

The previous reference of "color" not only represents separating people by ethnic groups but separating people by their different personalities as well. Whether or not a Sales Professional labels people by their skin color, personality-type

> The ego loves it when we label people instead of interacting with them as simply "another person".

by color, by labeling people like an animal, or any other way doesn't matter. The ego loves it when we label people like a "certain type", instead of interacting with them as simply "another person".

Let me be clear about the fact that there have been books written on identifying your customer's personality traits and interacting to them in their preferred way of communicating. Clearly, there is a definite advantage to speaking to customers in "their world of listening". The core issue here is that many Sales Professionals cannot control their thoughts enough to prevent their ego from twisting the labeling of people out of proportion. Therefore, what could be an advantage becomes a disadvantage – a double-edged sword.

Imagine what the world would be like without the ego?

Although the ego is found in every human being, some of the largest egos are found in Sales Professionals.

Some experts think it is because Sales Professionals are taught things in their selling career that tell them they need to be "better than everyone else" in order to be #1. Those thoughts help fuel their egos until they balloon out of proportion.

> Most Sales Professionals are taught to believe that they are better than everyone – they must be #1. These thoughts fuel the ego.

With everyday thoughts like this, the ego in their mind would blow out of proportion similar to how their body would blow out of proportion if they ate at an all-you-can-eat, resort-style buffet for every breakfast, lunch and dinner.

Overfilling the mind works the same as overfilling the body; both can get ugly.

For some unfortunate Sales Professionals, the ego becomes so large and overwhelming that they act arrogant and self-absorbed; the *exact opposite* of how they should act. In the worst cases, some Sales Professionals even act preoccupied and seem "put-out" simply because you are asking them questions about what they are selling, because they have already chosen not to work you and you have become a nuisance. These unfortunate Sales Professionals are so far gone that they don't even *know* it.

They set ego-based goals that are all about them, and reinforce their internal dialogue with, "I am the best!" Yet, ironically, it is their ego that _blocks their path_ and _prevents them_ from achieving the very goal that their ego set for them!

The ego is at the core of your challenges in achieving great success in sales.

This is contrary to your current beliefs about being "self-motivated", or possessing an "internal drive" that steers you towards great success. The irony here is that at the same time your ego is driving you to set ego-based goals, it is your ego that prevents you from achieving those goals.

It's ironic that your ego prevents you from achieving your fullest potential and prevents you from generating maximum sales.

Most likely, you have not read anything like the previous statement before. And most likely, you have believed all of your selling career that you needed a strong, internal drive for success, the drive to sell, sell, sell, and sell some more. I thought that same thought for nearly three decades. I was never happy, never satisfied, and I walked around frustrated thinking that was the way it was supposed to be – always be after more; <u>never be satisfied</u>. Thinking like that was the only thing I knew for most of my sales career.

Most people associate a person with a strong inner drive, always wanting to get more, as a person with a very large ego. This is only partially true. In this particular case, *it is not the size that matters*. It is simply the fact that when your ego, and not your intellect, drives you and sets your goals, it is your ego that messes you up; it plays you.

This information is so profound that it will change your life. The humor and cartoons were a creative way to get you here. Now that I have your attention, my desire is to share with you the following information so you can absorb it, apply it, and achieve self-fulfillment at the deepest level.

Of course, you will make a quantum leap in your sales achievements.

The ego is competitive. The ego always says, "I need more!"…it is *never* satisfied for any long term. Only temporary satisfaction results from ego-driven goals. You get an award plaque, and on the surface you feel great for a little while. Once that ego goal was accomplished, the need for another ego-driven goal overtakes you. The ego always tells you that you need more – <u>it is never satisfied</u>.

Therefore, you always live in a state of dissatisfaction. Living in a state of "I don't live the life I deserve" leaves no place for happiness. People that allow their egos to control them are unhappy people on the inside. They acquire something from the outside; *a thing* they thought would make them happy. But happiness from that thing is only temporary. The ego demands more.

Contrary to popular belief, your ego actually limits your feelings of success and self-achievement. Understand this very simple fact: if you achieved great success by achieving your ego-driven goals, and if you reached that place of self-fulfill-ment, that inner peace that you were working so hard for... your ego would not survive, simply because your ego would have no food to live on. The ego feeds on the feeling of dis-satisfaction. It is in constant hunger for more. In a state of "self-fulfillment", there is no food for your ego, and it would not survive.

Throughout the history of modern man, the ego has yet to be conquered, per-haps for one very simple reason: lack of awareness. Wisdom about the ego is not produced in our formal education system...partic-ularly in Western culture. The Middle and Far-Eastern cultures are more aware but still face great challenges.

Wisdom about the ego is not produced in our formal education system...particularly in Western culture.

Your ego will not drive you home down Happiness Lane, simply because the ego and happiness cannot live together. Einstein exhausted many years attempting to change that fact. He finally surrendered and went on to work on easier proj-ects.

There is a trap that I want you to recognize so you don't fall into it. If you are setting goals that require you to acquire enough material things in your life, which will allow you to someday look back and decide how happy you are at the end of the game ...and you allow your ego to consistently harass you and tell you that you are not acquiring things fast enough…can you really be happy living like that?

No wonder you may feel trapped, or "stuck".

But you ask, "What about you, the Sales Professional?" Don't you need your ego to drive you to more sales, and more sales? Isn't it your ego which fuels your motivation that will take you to the Sales Professional of the Year podium? Isn't it that internal drive, that self-motivation of yours which will allow you to increase your income, so you can start living a better life?

You may think that with no ego, you would have no goals… right?

All of those are false assumptions that ballooned out of proportion and have become a consensus with most Sales Professionals. There is a better way.

Let's revisit the part about your ego blocking you from reaching your highest Sales Achievements. The irony of all of this is that it is your ego that influences you to <u>not perform</u> a complete presentation sometimes.

Remember, your ego fuels your Cherry Picking thoughts. The following are some examples of how your ego plays you:

A customer comes to you just before lunch. <u>Reality</u> is, "This is a potential sale." But your ego is driving and alters your thinking. Your ego makes you think, "I am a great Sales Professional. This might be a good customer, but I don't want to deal with them now; I want to go to lunch. It's no big deal, because I am a great Sales Professional; I'll get another customer later and I'll just sell them." But later that day, no one shows.

Your ego smiles.

You did not make a complete presentation with that customer and you went to lunch. That customer, the one that you did a less-than-stellar presentation to, was *the one*. They buy from your competitor. The result is that you now live in lack of the sales you need. Your ego then harasses you that you need another sale. You are dissatisfied with your current sales; your ego is playing you.

You now think you are "self-motivated", so you set out to sell some more.

The next customer you get is a customer that has an "orange" personality. You prefer to work with blue people and purple people. Your ego tells you that you are "The Greatest Sales Professional" and you only have to work with people that you want to. Your ego is snickering at you because the reality is that you are a Sales Professional and you are supposed to be personality-blind. Reality is that your job is to perform a complete, planned presentation to <u>all people</u>; after all, <u>that's what they pay you for</u>.

"I'm not going to work these people...just look at 'em."

Your ego bullies your intellect. It tells you that you are a great Sales Professional and that you are so good that you only have to work with the people that you choose to. So you choose to <u>not</u> work with this orange person because you will sell a green one later. The end result is no sale...and you continue to live with the need to acquire more sales; you ego played you. You think that you just can't win.

When your ego fuels your Cherry Picking thoughts and makes you believe that you are so good that you can choose <u>when and to whom</u> that you want to make a complete, planned presentation, you are simply not living in reality. I could not tell you this in the beginning of this book. If you had starting reading this book and were not hooked into it so deeply, your ego would have told you to put it down. Your ego would have told you that reading about your ego limiting your success couldn't possibly be true because you are smarter than that.

Live in dissatisfaction and the ego feeds well and stays strong. It wants you to always believe that you need more *things* in order for you to be happy. But now, because I have your attention, now you have a fighting chance.

You can <u>take the keys</u> away from your ego. You can transform. When you release your ego-driven thoughts and goals, your ego will not be in control; therefore, your ego will not limit your success. You will then have unlimited power from your intellect, and your true inner self will drive you. You will be able to move forward into a life of inner peace and happiness - the fulfilling life that your ego only plays you for, but never lets you have.

And yes, without your ego you are allowed to live in a very nice home… and drive a nice car too! Want to travel? Not a problem. And as of this writing, they have not passed any laws that I know of preventing you from *saving* money. Without your ego, you <u>can</u> live in a life of abundance. You are not only allowed to enjoy all of what you accomplish, but you don't have to wait until someday to enjoy them — you can enjoy them right now.

Most likely, as a Sales Professional, your ego has been driving you for a long time. It drove me, so I can speak from personal experience. I am not telling you to throw your ego out of the car just yet; that may seem a bit too drastic. But pull over and change places with your ego. Don't let your ego drive…it doesn't know the way. It will <u>not</u> take you down Reality Road or Happiness Lane.

Instead, your ego will take you on an exhausting, long-way-around trip that will keep you stressed and on-edge. And when you finally get to where your ego has taken you, you feel "beat-up".

My forthcoming book, <u>Attract vs. Attack</u>, identifies the false, ego-based goals that most Sales Professionals attempt to work from. Instead of setting ego-based goals that use negative energy and are short-lived, the book shows you how to set *creative-based* goals that expend an abundance of positive energy and are far more powerful and long-lasting.

While the ego is the leading factor for fueling thoughts of Cherry Picking, there is another "mental condition" that prevents Sales Professionals from selling to their fullest capacity. While the previously mentioned challenges will take a great effort on your part to conquer, the following challenge should be a much easier thing to tackle.

This mental condition is called *"not being present"*. The body is present, but the mind is not.

Must Be Present to Sell

You are probably familiar with the saying, "Must be present to win." So goes the sales game – must be present to sell. Sales Professionals need to be selling in the present moment, present with the current customer they are working with in order to receive the grand prize — "The Sale". This concept may sound simple...but doesn't "eat a little less, and exercise a little" also sound simple?

Millions of people complain about the shape they're in. Millions of people also cannot stay in the present moment for very long. Both of the former require <u>awareness</u> and <u>conscious thought</u>.

Some Sales Professionals choose when and to whom they will make a complete presentation to as their thoughts bounce them from the present to the past and the future.

When you watch some of them, you can see that much like a pinball, their thoughts randomly bounce from being present, to thinking about the past or the future.

One example is when a Sales Professional drives to work and decides on the drive that they do *not* want to do any complete presentations that day at all because it would be too time consuming - they couldn't get anything else done. They think that it is early in the month, and they would rather get their administrative work done for the month. Then, the Sales Professional would be freed-up to sell the rest of the month. To me, the obvious flaw of this thinking is the fact that there is a huge assumption made here, that the right qualified customers will hold-off since it is early in the month and will wait for the Sales Professional to get their work done. Then, when it is convenient for the Sales Professional, the customers will walk in.

The Sales Professional is not present; they are thinking about how much better it would be for them to sell one day in the future when they are clear of this other stuff they have to do, so they do <u>not</u> sell today - in the present.

A real-life example of how not being present can kill a sale is the time I had a new home Sales Professional tell me that she was almost "sold out" in that particular community and that she would be moving soon to a new location. She mentioned that there were only three lots left in the community we were in…but by her tone and with the way she said it, she made it sound like she didn't have *any* lots left. Her demeanor was that there was *nothing* to buy there *today* – that she was done selling until she moved – which was *some day* in the future.

But reality was that she had *three lots* to sell, and in reality, I was only going to buy *one*. I only needed <u>one lot</u> so I could build my <u>one home</u> on it! I was a customer in the present moment and she was walking around almost unconscious in a daydream about some day in the future!

Unfortunately, the list is rather long of other examples of how Sales Professionals do not sell in the present moment. They will have a ready, willing, and able customer standing in front of them, but because they *know* that during "the winter", or "back to school time", or "tax time", it is really slow, they completely ignore reality and do not sell in the present moment. Their ego influences their thoughts, bullies their intellect by telling them that they know better, and blocks their path to making a sale.

The ego laughs again. With no sales, they "gotta get more sales!" The number of times this happens each year is unknown, but the estimates are very high. However, there is good news.

Now that you know the cause of Cherry Picking, what fuels your Cherry Picking thoughts and creates your selective selling habits, you can learn about the solution. There is a remedy that is showing promising results, one that is far better than the Sales Manager's Prescription. You are now ready to learn about what specific actions to take in the next chapter.

Knowledge is Power.

Chapter Highlights

- **If you are told that you will sell one in X, human nature might make you look for "*the one*".**

- **Your ego plays you.**

- **Unfortunately, there is little to no formal education about the ego.**

- **Sales Professionals are taught to believe that they are #1, and that they are better than everyone else. This fuels the ego.**

- **You *can* live in a nice home, travel, and be very successful without the ego.**

SIX

The Cure

I hope that you have enjoyed this book so far, and I hope that you will share it with someone. We have looked at some pretty serious material in a fun way. The point of it all was for you to get it. You now understand the enormous cost of Cherry Picking. Now, let's do something about it.

In this portion of the book, we have to get serious, because this is the opportunity for you to change not only your Sales Performance, but quite literally, change your life. When you apply what you learn in this section, you will see profound changes in all areas of your life. Your relationships with your customers, family, friends — and most importantly, your relationship with *you* — will radiate from your deepest inner level.

I am a seasoned Sales Professional. I sold big tickets for 20+ years before starting my own company. The amount of income I lost due to Cherry Picking will never be known. I was blessed early in my career and acquired some knowledge about Cherry Picking, so my total losses were somewhat limited, but I wish I was handed a check today for all of my lost income from Cherry Picking.

I have helped count-less people across North America understand the significance of practicing and performing their com-plete, planned presentation with every customer. To help captivate and retain attention, I deliver some

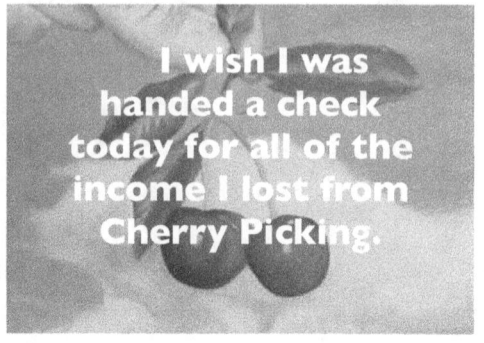

material with humor… as if you haven't already noticed. In Reflection Selling Workshops, Sales Professionals and Sales Managers walk away stimulated to take the actions necessary to generate maximum sales.

When a Sales Professional gets in tune with that internal, positive energy source that flows from the inside out, they radiate…that's when they perform their "A Game" presentation.

People buy from happy people with positive energy.

Early in my life, I was blessed and enlightened to some concepts of better selling. Later on, I was enlightened to con-cepts of better living. You really want to slow down here and get this.

When you set ego-based goals, such as, "I need to sell x, and *then* I will be happy," you place your feeling of accomplish-ment, your day of being happy on…*someday*. You then turn your goals into hurdles that you must jump over in order for you to *someday* relax and be happy. And of course, your ego constantly nags you that you're in a race against a lot of others.

What is happening *in your mind* is that you live in a competitive world, and you're in a tough race. It appears that there are a lot of high hurdles for you to jump over, so *in your mind*, today and a lot of tomorrows need to get out of your way. You want *someday* to get here so will have accomplished something, because *only then* you can look back, relax, and be happy.

There is only one basic, scientific fact about this: when you get to that future *someday* that you dream about…when you are living in *that day*… it will be a *today*. In reality, there is no past and there is no future, they are <u>only in your mind</u>. You only have *today*.

Your ego loves to make you think thoughts like "If you had only done it differently in the past, you would be somewhere different now", and "You will definitely be somewhere better in the future than where you are now". Your ego loves to keep you thinking like that, for one simple reason: you can't change it or do anything about it! As a result, you feel out of control; you feel "trapped".

Your subconscious mind carries the weight of these negative inner feelings about yourself and how you measure yourself *today*. And those ego-based goals that you have set for yourself but never achieve? They only add to your frustration. Your ego tells you to "overachieve" in the morning, and calls you "an underachiever" at night. The ego has a sick sense of humor.

Inside your mind, subconscious energy is constantly being burned about you missing your goals and your life not working out the way you want it to. Your thoughts about this may spark to the surface periodically when something doesn't go the way you thought it should, and you say, "Of course, that figures, I just can't win."

You then need reasons why you feel that you are not living the life that you deserve, and why you just "can't win". And those reasons why you just can't win are reasons that your ego alters into convincing you that they are <u>external reasons</u>. Of course, *in your mind*, as a Sales Professional, your ego convinces you that those external reasons are beyond your control…things like a lack of qualified prospects to work with, your prices and/or features are not right, etc. Of course you just can't win! I'm exhausted just writing about it.

Can you imagine living that way? It's sad and unfortunate, but many people do.

It's no wonder that you might feel stressed, trapped, and "just can't win". The ego is so strong in Western culture that many Americans have adopted the saying "I just can't win", and it's now become a cultural phenomenon. The irony is  that whatever the person feels so frustrated about and says, "I just can't win" is probably something that if they would just let a little time pass, the person would view it differently and they wouldn't be so emotionally charged about it. This exaggerated frustration, which is negative energy, is the ego's sick sense of humor. It beats you up.

You can think of it this way: the types of negative thoughts that drain your energy are similar to an appliance that draws constant power. Even when an appliance is turned off it still uses up energy. So do negative thoughts in your subconscious. Even though you are not engaged in negative self-talk, the fact is that those negative thoughts of frustration and living in dissatisfaction in your subconscious mind are always expending your energy.

Let's face it, you only have X amount of total energy. By living in a constant state of not having enough, which burns negative energy, and by living in a state of feeling trapped in your life and not knowing what to do, all of those types of negative thoughts in your subconscious drain your energy. That is why people love vacations, and have their favorite places that they say will "recharge their batteries".

What happens in those favorite places?

What happens in those favorite places is that your positive, internal talk of "life is good," overrides your negative thoughts. Your positive thoughts are stronger, and generate lots of energy that you feel is uplifting. You feel better.

Most people, that is.

Unfortunately, some people cannot even control their own thoughts enough to allow them to enjoy their time off. How sad but true.

"Last week was horrible. Next week will be even worse."

To date, most motivational sales materials are ego-based. The strategies may tickle the Sales Soul, but the tingle is short-lived. The reason is that the underlying core, the foundation of the energy expended, the *ego energy*, is negative energy. The ego leaves you feeling dissatisfied.

To date, you have probably been taught to make all of your goals ego-based.

The core reason why you Cherry Pick is simply human nature. Those original small, petty thoughts are then fueled by your ego. The reasons why you choose to perform a complete, planned presentation or <u>not to</u> are influenced by your ego.

The solution to change is simple…but not easy.

For the previous behavior to change, <u>your intellect needs to be in control</u>. You need to focus and be conscious of your thoughts. The sooner you take the keys away from your ego, the less wrong turns you will make, and the faster you will get to where you want to go. Your intellect, your true inner self, will take you on the scenic route of life. And there are lots of places to stop on the scenic route to soak up some positive energy, and recharge your batteries.

This information will not only be the cause for you to see immediate results in your Sales Performance, but it will remove stress from your life; it will feel as if a heavy backpack is taken off your shoulders. It might take reading this information a couple of times for it to sink in.

I want to make clear one final point…the previous mentioned *positive energy* that you will experience is not from an <u>external </u>source. In other words, you do not need an extension cord thousands of miles long so you can plug into some positive energy source that is far off in the universe somewhere. It's quite the contrary.

Think about when you go into nature. Hopefully, at some time in your life, you have been to the mountains or into a forest; somewhere outside of the city, beyond billboards and neon signs. There are a lot of beaches where you can achieve the same result of what I am about to share.

When you were at that special place, you hit the pause button on your hectic life. In fact, you may view going to these special places as having "time-out for *you*". In essence, you feel as if you *bought the clock* for a while.

At this special place, when you allow your mind to settle and as your mind relaxes, you sense something. You feel a positive energy deep inside you. And that's the point exactly...it is inside you; it is <u>internal</u> and not <u>external</u>.

The positive energy originates at a deep level inside you.

First, it saturates your soul. Then, that positive energy radiates outward. Label it anything that you want; it is simply an internal source of positive energy that originates from deep inside you, and then radiates outward.

This energy that radiates outward is the reason why you may say that someone looks so happy that they seem to be "glowing." That is true simply because they are happy on the inside and their happiness is projected outward.

People buy from happy, positive people.

Remember, people buy from happy, positive, people.

As I mentioned earlier, the ego and your happiness cannot live together inside you. Look at it this way: a light bulb in a closet turned "off" makes the closet dark. Instead of shining a light into the closet to see, you turn the light bulb in the closet on. Now the light shines from inside the closet – outward. In fact, there now may be enough light radiating from within the closet that you see things outside of the closet…perhaps the entire room!

Consider that your internal, positive energy is the light "on", and it shines from within you – outward. That is why when a Sales Professional gets into a positive mental state, they say that they are now "on" their game. It is at this time that they plan to make *complete, planned presentations* - and make a sale.

When you replace your negative energy and turn on the positive energy, you not only sell that way, but you live that way as well. Instead of waiting for the good life to happen *someday*, you will enjoy what you have *today* — and your life will change, *today*.

Instead of setting ego-based, "I must" do this so "I can" have that goals… set goals that will fill your life with positive energy. Think about how you are going to create a new lifestyle for your next customer, and how they will benefit from your product or service, and how they will enjoy it. When you shift your focus and sell that way, your life will change… and you will enjoy *today*.

Relax a little and enjoy life – *today*. You can fulfill your "Life's Purpose" by not looking so hard for it. Living in frustration about not understanding your true "Life's Purpose" will simply expend negative energy and waste your valuable resources. You'll never find "IT". Your ego is playing you. It's your ego's sick sense of humor.

Remember that you learned earlier that your ego makes you feel different from others. So it makes perfect sense for your ego to influence you to believe that you have some unfound, unique destiny...your individual "Life's Purpose". You are convinced that it can only belong to you...because you are separate from all others.

Just who exactly is going to tell you that you have found your "Life's Purpose"? Your preacher, your teacher, your parents, a sibling, your boss, your best friend...who do you think you will believe when they tell you that you have found your "Life's Purpose"?

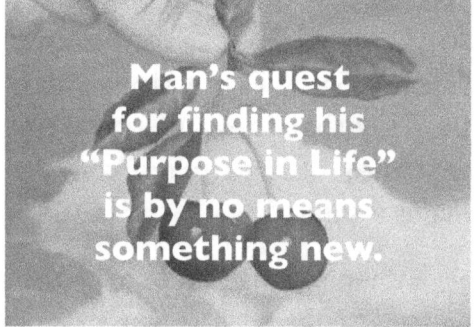

Man's quest for finding his "Purpose in Life" is by no means something new.

By the way, the endless quest for finding your "Purpose in Life" is by no means something new. Man has been looking for his purpose ever since he could communicate that thought to himself. Finding your purpose in life is only a matter of changing your internal dialogue. It is simply a matter of being at peace with your internal beliefs.

Instead of living with not enough and needing more, you could decide one day that you live in a life of abundance. Perhaps one day you might visit a foreign country...just visit the back side of Cozumel Island, away from the development for tourists, and see the people there living in grass huts. In an instant, all of the last year's worth of thoughts about you not having enough is washed away. In an instant, you realize that you live in a life of abundance.

But your ego travels with you. It returns home with you, and the moment you step off the plane it harasses you about not having enough, and pesters you on why you haven't found your Life's Purpose.

When you live with positive energy that radiates from the inside out, you might "glow" and light up a room, and you might not. But by simply being happy deep inside, your "Life's Purpose" will become clear; I have yet to learn of anyone that didn't have that happen.

Here is a three-step process of something that will make you feel happy deep within you; you can do it from right where you are now. You can make this your special place for this exercise:

1. Close your eyes and repeat inside your mind, "I choose to live in positive energy." You may have to repeat it 10-15-20 times; repeat it as many as you have to. "I choose to live in positive energy." You will know when you shift to generating positive energy because without your command, the positive energy will acti- vate a smile. It's called "an automated response". It's like when the doctor hits your knee and your foot kicks up without you telling it to.

After you smile, go to step 2.

2. Now that you are generating positive energy, picture that in 10 minutes you are leaving earth...permanently.

Accept that you are not ever coming back. Intelligent beings from somewhere far away in the universe have just contacted you and selected you as *the one*. You are the one in X humans they have chosen, and they are on their way to get you. You are going to be beamed up to their spacecraft with just the clothes that you have on. For all of the women readers…picture putting the suitcases down. You really have to leave with just what you have on.

Please stay focused.

Of course you are shocked in disbelief, and your emotions are overwhelming. It would simply be human nature for you to feel anxious. You have accepted that you really are leaving earth in just 10 minutes, and now you panic over who you need to call.

Go ahead and mentally make a short list, or write it out on paper, of who you would call. But remember, you only have 10 minutes to talk. You will probably have to appoint a spokesperson that will say some goodbyes for you on your behalf. Think about which friend or family member that might be, and think about what you want them to say.

Think about to whom you might want to make amends with and that you need to quickly call them yourself. When you are done with whom you choose to call and what you want to say, go to step 3.

3. Now imagine that the aliens are beaming you up, and as you are leaving earth and looking back, ask yourself this question: As you leave earth, what are you going to miss? Is it the furniture you owned, the car you drove, or any other material thing? Or is it the people that were in your life? Perhaps it is one of those special vacation places where you felt like you "bought the clock" and recharged your batteries?

Just as you are about to enter the spacecraft, as a final thought, who or what is it that you would miss the most?

Think about this, and be very clear about it before you continue.

Now, right at this time, right when you realize what you will miss the most, the intelligent beings inform you that where they live, no egos are allowed. Their culture lives without ego. Their species became aware of the limited view the ego allows, and they called it out and banished it from their cultural conscious.

The aliens inform you that they had to extract your ego while they were beaming you up, so you may feel light-headed.

Actually, what just happened is that while you were being beamed up and were reflecting back about your life on earth, your perspective on what was important to you and what you were going to miss was with a clear view from your inner self. You looked at your life with a clear view and without the influence of ego. That is why everything appeared different to you. That is why you did not feel that what you would miss was any material things.

Of course, it all makes sense now, because you have heard it a million times before you read this material…all of those material things really don't matter, and they really don't make you happy. And you definitely can't take them with you.

But right at this moment, the intelligent beings tell you that something has just happened at the other end, and they can't take you right now. They have to beam you back down.

They say they will come back and get you someday soon, but they are not sure when. They quickly zap you right back where they took you from.

I need to inform you here of a really unpleasant thought; I don't want to, but I have to do it. You need to understand something here…the previously mentioned intelligent beings that were taking you to their place? Remember, you're a human that all throughout your life have allowed your ego to influence your thinking…you would have not ever fit in at their place!

Actually, the aliens' intention was never to select you as the one to come live with them. Actually, you were selected as the one to be <u>a lab project</u> for them.

They were going to dissect your brain so they could answer questions like, "Why are humans destroying the blue planet? Humans have powerful telescopes now, and they have seen that the majority of other planets are bare and desolate places, so why do humans allow their egos to drive them to the point of destroying the beautiful blue planet…all because they think they need more things?"

The aliens wonder why the human species has been in existence for so long, yet they live on a planet that is two-thirds water and claim they have a water shortage. They waste vast resources on war and political campaigns as opposed to inventing the technology to simply take salt out of sea water.

The supreme beings are very concerned with humans becoming aware of how the universe was created. They have monitored the most recent experiments that humans are conducting on particle acceleration and nuclear fission, and are very concerned, and justifiably so.

The supreme beings have also observed some rather bizarre actions performed by humans. For example, if it is a known fact that better Sales Presentations to more customers will generate more sales – then why would a Sales Professional choose not to perform a complete presentation to a customer for just enne ol' reason? And then complain that they don't have enough?

It wasn't going to be a party for you. The supreme, intelligent beings were going to poke and prod you to death looking for the answer to these questions. They feel that if humans cannot control their thoughts enough and think straight when it comes to something as simple as doing what they were hired to do – perform a complete sales presentation on every customer – then most definitely the power of the workings of the universe cannot be put in their hands.

Humans must be enlightened to the destructive power of the ego. They must become aware of it now at this critical time in their evolution. The very survival of the human species is at risk, yet many humans, especially in the Western cultures, are only concerned with what manufactured things make them look better than each other as they live in paradise – the blue planet.

From the outside looking in, this appears insane.

The aliens were going to dissect your brain to find the answers they were looking for simply because you could not have answered their questions. You just did not know what you did not know. You were not aware of how your ego has been playing you – until now.

Think about how your perspective on your life would be different without the influence of your ego.

After reading this, you have become aware.

Think about what has just happened.

Think about how your perspective changed on the things that really matter to you as you were leaving them behind. But this makes perfect sense because you have heard many times before that you never appreciate something until it's taken away. You always want what you don't have.

Think about how your clear view of your life – without the influence of ego — makes you feel. People tell me that it is profoundly different for them.

Again, it all makes sense now because you have heard it before – "You can't take it with you, and enjoy every day as if it was your last."

End of exercise.

Let's revisit a previously mentioned thought. You realize that you can make your plan that *someday* you will *enjoy life*. But you know that *someday* you won't be on earth, and you don't know *what day* that *someday* is.

It is possible that you might feel a little differently now. Just think that when the aliens beamed you back, they forgot to give you back your ego. Don't be alarmed - your family, friends, and co-workers have enough egos to rekindle old thoughts...they are anchored in your brain and you can't just delete them.

But you are now aware, and what that means is that without your ego influencing your decisions on *when and to whom* you will perform a *complete, planned presentation*, perhaps <u>today is the turnaround for you</u>.

Today, you can perform a complete, planned presentation on *every* customer.

Today is not only the beginning of more sales for you, but more importantly, along with enjoying those sales, you will enjoy a better life as well.

Cherry Picking. How much does it...rather, *did it* cost you?

I like happy endings. Consider this: if you undo your Cherry Picking and conquer your selective selling habits today, how much "Found Money" will come into your life? You will see when you fill in the "Found Money" chart following.

Found Money in the Next 12 Months

_____Cherry Picks from previous chapter because of *Peek Qualifying*

+_____Cherry Picks from previous chapter because of *Enne 'ol Reezon*

=_____GRAND TOTAL of all Cherry Picks

X_____Average commission

$_____Grand total of Found Money in the next 12 months

Chapter Highlights

- When a Sales Professional radiates with positive energy, they perform on their "A" game. People buy from happy, positive people.

- You can fulfill your "Life's Purpose" by not looking so hard for it.

- The cure is to identify your ego and don't let it bully your intellect.

- By selling Cherry Picking-free, imagine how much found money will come into your life!

SEVEN

The Close

ou saw how much Cherry Picking costs you. You learned how the ego fuels Cherry Picking thoughts. Simply *identify* your ego, call it out, and it will be powerless over you. When you know that your ego is driving, pay attention to where it is taking you. When you see a place to pull over, you make your ego stop and trade places – you drive. Let your higher inner self — *your intellect* — drive, and you will enjoy the ride.

As you drive along the highway of self-fulfillment, stay focused and stay present. Stop along the way at the lookout points and absorb the incredible views. You let your intellect drive you down Reality Road, and turn down your street, Happiness Lane. You have now bought the clock, but for far longer than previous vacations of just a week or two; you have bought the clock of life.

If you want to learn more about owning the clock of life, read my upcoming book, <u>Attract vs. Attack…Attraction Wins Every Time</u>.

How unfortunate that most people have to be next to death in order to feel life without their ego influencing and altering their thoughts. While close to death, they enjoy a clear view of their life here on earth. It is only in those few brief and final moments that the struggle to be "better", and to be "right", melts away. Their frustration, because of the need to acquire more things to make them happy, is no longer felt because it no longer matters. They realize in their last, final thoughts what was really important to them – then the aliens beam them up and they are gone.

But you, the fortunate one, you get to put your feet on the floor and go perform a complete, planned presentation and sell the next one. Better selling, better living; you get to live and enjoy another day. You have – *today*.

Please share this with someone. The dynamic of this material changes from simply thinking thoughts about it to having conversations about it.

Sell one.

ABOUT THE AUTHOR

Mike Jackson is the founder of Progressive Insights, Inc., a Sales Training and Personal Development organization. His company supports and enhances the Sales Training and Personal Development efforts of Fortune 500 companies.

Mike authored the Reflection Selling Program, a comprehensive Sales Training and Personal Development Program. Mike has trained countless Sales Professionals across North America, and is a leading expert in Selling Strategies and Personal Development for Sales Professionals, Sales Managers and Business Owners.

To order more copies of

CHERRY PICKING

Visit your favorite bookstore

Or call 1-888-326-3722

Or visit CherryPicking.me

www.ingramcontent.com/pod-product-compliance
Lightning Source LLC
Chambersburg PA
CBHW051547170526
45165CB00002B/914